Understanding the

SACRAMENTS
of HEALING

A Rite-Based Approach

RANDY STICE

LITURGY
TRAINING
PUBLICATIONS

Nihil Obstat
Very Reverend Daniel A. Smilanic, JCD
Vicar for Canonical Services
Archdiocese of Chicago
May 21, 2015

Imprimatur
Very Reverend Ronald A. Hicks
Vicar General
Archdiocese of Chicago
May 21, 2015

UNDERSTANDING THE SACRAMENTS OF HEALING: A RITE-BASED APPROACH © 2015 Archdiocese of Chicago: Liturgy Training Publications, 3949 South Racine Avenue, Chicago, IL 60609; 1-800-933-1800, fax 1-800-933-7094, e-mail orders@ltp.org, website: www.ltp.org.

This book was edited by Kevin Thornton. Christian Rocha was the production editor, Anna Manhart was the designer, and Luis Leal was the production artist.

Printed in the United States of America.

Library of Congress Control Number: 2015946393

19   18   17   16   15   1   2   3   4   5

ISBN: 978-1-61671-249-5

USH

CONTENTS

FOREWORD

During my fifteen years of priesthood, many of my most powerful pastoral experiences have occurred as a minister of the Church's two sacraments of healing: Penance and Anointing of the Sick. A man enters the confessional after many years away from the practice of his faith and joyfully emerges, having been forgiven and restored in his relationships with Lord, with the community, and within himself. A seriously ill woman preparing for major surgery, her hospital bed surrounded by family and friends, is anointed and receives peace, hope, and strength through an encounter with the crucified and risen Lord.

The purpose of the sacraments of healing, according to the Church, is as follows: "The Lord Jesus Christ, physician of our souls and bodies . . . has willed that his Church continue, in the power of the Holy Spirit, his work of healing and salvation, even among her own members" (*Catechism of the Catholic Church*, 1421). In the words of St. Paul, we carry the new life received in the sacraments of initiation in "earthen vessels" (2 Cor 4:7). We are subject to suffering, sickness, and, ultimately, death as we make this earthly pilgrimage. Our new life as an adopted child of the Father can be weakened or even lost through sin. The sacraments of healing are the gifts entrusted by God to the Church to bring healing and transformation in these varied circumstances. They are, like the other sacraments, personal encounters that draw us more deeply into the mystery of communion with the Holy Trinity.

In this new volume, Father Randy Stice offers us an excellent study of these two sacraments of healing deeply rooted in the testimony of Sacred Scripture and the teaching of the Church. Through the liturgical rites and sacramental symbols themselves, he explores in a rich yet understandable way the power of Reconciliation and Anointing in the lives of Christian disciples. This work reflects the theological acumen and pastoral experience of its author. Father Stice's labors will surely bear fruit in bringing many of us, whether as ministers or recipients, to a more profound experience of God's healing gifts in the sacraments.

Father Ronald Kunkel, STL, STD
University of St. Mary of the Lake/Mundelein Seminary

ABBREVIATIONS

CB	*Ceremonial of Bishops*	NABRE	*New American Bible, Revised Edition*
CCC	*Catechism of the Catholic Church*	PCS	*Pastoral Care of the Sick*
DiM	*Dives in Misericordia*	PMDM	*The Priest, Minister of Divine Mercy*
EE	*Ecclesia de Eucharistia*		
EG	*Evangelii Gaudium*	PO	*Presbyterorum Ordinis*
EM	*Eucharisticum Mysterium* (Instruction on the Worship of the Eucharistic Mystery)	RBC	*Rite of Baptism of Children*
		RP	*Rite of Penance*
GICI	*General Introduction to Christian Initiation*	RaP	*Reconciliation and Penance*
		RM	*Roman Missal*
GIRM	*General Instruction of the Roman Missal*	RO	*Rite of Ordination*
		SacCar	*Sacramentum Caritatis*
GS	*Gaudium et Spes*	SC	*Sacrosanctum Concilium*
ID	*Indulgentiarum Doctrina*	SD	*Salvifici Doloris (On the Christian Meaning of Human Suffering)*
IOM	*Introduction to the Order of Mass*		
LI	*Liturgiae Instaurationes*		
MC	*Mystici Corporis*	SL	*Sing to the Lord*
MI	*Manual of Indulgences*	VD	*Verbum Domini*
MND	*Mane Nobiscum Domine*	VQA	*Vicesimus Quintus Annus*
MS	*Musicam Sacram* (Instruction on Music in the Liturgy)	VL	*Varietates Legitimae*
		VS	*Veritatis Splendor*

General Introduction

"Behold, I am with you always, until the end of the age."

Matthew 28:20

Before Jesus ascended to the Father, he promised the apostles that he would remain with them always. The Seven Sacraments of the Church—Baptism, Confirmation, Eucharist, Penance and Reconciliation, Anointing of the Sick, Holy Orders, Matrimony—are the primary ways that Jesus continues to fulfill the promise of his abiding presence. In Christ, every sacrament is an encounter with the Trinity: "A sacramental celebration is a meeting of God's children with their Father, in Christ and the Holy Spirit" (CCC, 1153). While various approaches and disciplines such as history, sociology, anthropology, psychology, semiotics, and ritual can deepen our understanding and experience of the sacraments, these approaches are secondary and build on what is primary—the personal encounter with the Trinity.

This Trinitarian sacramental encounter is a "dialogue" that uses both "actions and words" that together constitute "a language" (CCC, 1153). Like any language, this sacramental language has its own vocabulary, grammar, and syntax that must be learned if one is to enter into the sacramental dialogue with the Father in Christ and the Holy Spirit. The aim of this book is to explore and master the language of the sacraments, looking in detail at the sacraments of healing—Penance and Anointing of the Sick—so that we can participate fully, consciously and actively in this dialogue with the Trinity through the words and actions of the sacramental celebration.

TRINITARIAN

While Christ's institution of and action through the sacraments is rightly stressed, it is important to always remember and explore the Trinitarian dimension of the sacraments. "We are called to be a dwelling for the Most Holy Trinity: 'If a man loves me,' says the Lord, 'he will keep my word, and my Father will love him, and we will come to

1

him, and make our home with him' [Jn 14:23]" (CCC, 260). The work of
the Trinity in creation and salvation, what is known as "the divine
economy," is performed jointly by the three divine persons, although
each divine person contributes to the common work "according to his
unique personal property" (CCC, 258). If we don't affirm the distinction of the persons, we deny that God is a trinity of persons, and if we
don't affirm the unity and common work of the three persons, we profess three gods, not one. Throughout this volume I will delineate the
activity of each divine person in the common work of the sacraments
so that we can experience in our lives what the *Catechism* affirms, that
"the whole Christian life is a communion with each of the divine persons, without in any way separating them" (CCC, 259).

TERMINOLOGY

Throughout this work you will encounter references not only to the
sacraments but also to the liturgy, to liturgical celebrations as well as
sacramental celebrations. The terms *liturgy* and *sacrament* are overlap-
ping but not synonymous. *Liturgy* as it is used in this book is the more
inclusive term, referring to the official public worship of the Church for
which there are official ritual books. It includes the Seven Sacraments,
but also such celebrations as the blessings found in the *Book of Blessings*,
the *Liturgy of the Hours*, and the *Rite of Christian Initiation for Adults*.
Sacrament is a narrower term that refers just to the Seven Sacraments of
the Church. Everything said of the liturgy or liturgical celebrations is
true of the sacraments, but references to the sacraments or sacramental
celebrations are not necessarily true of nonsacramental liturgical celebrations such as those taken from the *Book of Blessings* or the *Liturgy of
the Hours*. The *Catechism's* summary concisely characterizes the relationship between the liturgy and the sacraments: "The whole liturgical
life of the Church revolves around the Eucharistic sacrifice and the sacraments" (CCC, 1113).

Rite-Based

As the title indicates, my approach in this volume is rite-based. The rite
itself is always the best starting point, for these are the words we hear
and say, the gestures and postures we adopt, and the signs and symbols
that engage us. In addition, the liturgy is one of the primary ways that

the Church has passed on the faith entrusted to her by the Lord. Christ has entrusted to the Church the responsibility of passing "on the faith in its integrity so that the 'rule of prayer' (*lex orandi*) of the church may correspond to the 'rule of faith' (*lex credendi*)" (VL, 27). The terms "rule of prayer" (*lex orandi*) and "rule of faith" (*lex credendi*) refer to a principle that dates back to Prosper of Aquitaine (fifth century). "The law of prayer is the law of faith: the Church believes as she prays. Liturgy is a constitutive element of the holy and living Tradition" (CCC, 1124). St. Irenaeus (late second century) expressed this principle with respect to the Mass: "Our way of thinking is attuned to the Eucharist, and the Eucharist in turn confirms our way of thinking" (CCC, 1327). From the earliest days the Church has understood the inseparable relationship between her worship and her faith, and for this reason the sacramental rite is always the best starting point for understanding the meaning of the sacrament itself.

Sources

Since our approach is rite-based, our most important source will be the rite itself, which includes not only the words and actions of the rite but also the biblical readings for each of the sacraments. In addition, the Roman Missal contains ritual masses for the celebration of the sacraments within the Mass (with the exception of the Sacrament of Penance and Reconciliation), and these texts (e.g., prayers, prefaces, and solemn blessings) are also part of the sacramental rite. We will supplement the words and actions of the rite with selected other sources. The most frequently cited source is the *Catechism of the Catholic Church*, which St. John Paul II called "a sure and authentic reference text for teaching Catholic doctrine" and which he offered "to all the faithful who wish to deepen their knowledge of the unfathomable riches of salvation (cf. Eph 3:8)" (*Fidei Depositum*). Its presentation of the Catholic faith, illumined by Sacred Scripture, the writings of the saints, and the teaching of councils and popes, make it a rich and invaluable source of information on the sacraments. Readers of this book are encouraged to have a copy of the *Catechism of the Catholic Church* at hand. It is also available online at the Vatican website.

We will also make reference to the documents of the Second Vatican Council (1962–1965), which made the reform and restoration of the liturgy its first priority in the *Constitution on the Sacred Liturgy* (*Sacrosanctum Concilium*). These foundational documents will be supplemented by papal writings, St. John Paul II's apostolic exhortation *Reconciliation and Penance* and his apostolic letter *On the Christian Meaning of Human Suffering*, as well as Pope Benedict XVI's apostolic exhortations, *The Sacrament of Charity* (*Sacramentum Caritatis*) and *The Word of the Lord* (*Verbum Domini*). We will also have occasion to cite documents produced by Vatican congregations, such as the *The Priest, Minister of Divine Mercy* produced by the Congregation for the Clergy. Finally, we will also listen to the saints, especially the Church Fathers from the early centuries of the Church. We will also refer to works by contemporary theologians, liturgists, and historians.

As these sources suggest, we are not engaged in a speculative work of theology, nor are we proposing a new theory of the sacraments. Rather, our goal is to listen—attentively and prayerfully—to the voice of Christ and his Church in order to deepen our sacramental encounter with the Trinity.

Methodology

In this book we are using a method of sacramental catechesis described by Pope Emeritus Benedict XVI in his apostolic exhortation the *Sacrament of Charity* (*Sacramentum Caritatis*). This type of catechesis is called *mystagogy*, from the Greek word for the person who led an initiate into a mystery. Its goal is to lead people from the signs of the sacrament to the spiritual realities they signify. Pope Emeritus Benedict XVI proposes looking at three aspects of a sacrament:

1. The Old Testament origins of the sacrament
2. The meaning of the signs and symbols which comprise the sacrament
3. The meaning of the sacrament for whole of one's life
   (living the sacrament)

We will examine in detail each of these three aspects of the Sacraments of Penance and Anointing of the Sick by looking closely at the various elements of the rite and the different sources described above.

Organization

The book is divided into three parts. In part 1, we will briefly delve into an introduction to sacramental theology, consisting of chapters 1–3. Chapter 1 examines the different ways in which the Trinity is present in a sacramental celebration. Chapter 2 looks at the different sacramental signs that comprise the celebration. Chapter 3 introduces the method of mystagogical catechesis using examples from different sacraments to illustrate first the Old Testament roots, then the meaning of sacramental signs and symbols, and finally the comprehensive transformative power of the sacraments as we live sacramental lives. While the focus of this book is on the sacraments of healing, the examples in part 1 are drawn from the Sacraments of Baptism, Eucharist, Confirmation, and Holy Orders in order to provide the reader with some catechesis on all Seven Sacraments, not just the sacraments of Penance and the Anointing of the Sick.

Part 2 is a presentation of the Sacrament of Penance. Chapter 4 traces the Old Testament origins of this sacrament, chapter 5 analyzes the signs and symbols of the sacrament, and chapter 6 explores the meaning of Penance as a lived experience. Part 3 looks at the Sacrament of the Anointing of the Sick, following the same structure as part 2: Chapter 7 treats the Old Testament roots, chapter 8 examines the meaning of the constituent elements of the sacrament, and chapter 9 looks at the lived experience of the sacramental life. Chapter 10 reflects on the Sacraments of Penance and Anointing of the Sick as sacraments of healing.

AUDIENCE AND USE / ACTIVITIES

This book can be used by individuals as well as groups. It is primarily intended as a resource for those who are involved in preparing others for reception of the Sacraments of Penance and Anointing of the Sick. It is also appropriate for some religious education classes, adult faith formation, deaconate programs, undergraduate sacraments classes, and even high school sacraments classes. To facilitate its use in class or group settings, each chapter includes a number of different activities. These activities are intended to help the reader review and synthesize the material, explore a given topic in more detail (in some cases using the *Catechism of the Catholic Church*), and aid the reader in deepening his or her experience of the liturgy.

THE PRIVILEGED PLACE FOR ENCOUNTER

Although we encounter God in many different ways, "the Liturgy is the privileged place for the encounter of Christians with God and the one whom he has sent, Jesus Christ" (cf. Jn 17:3) (VQA, 7). It is there that "all Christian prayer finds its source and goal. Through the liturgy the inner man is rooted and grounded in 'the great love with which [the Father] loved us' in his beloved Son. It is the same 'marvelous work of God' that is lived and internalized by all prayer, 'at all times in the Spirit'" (CCC, 1073). It is my hope that this work will assist the reader in participating in the celebration of the Sacraments of Penance and Anointing of the Sick as privileged places of encounter with the Blessed Trinity, experiencing there the Father's love for us in Christ, poured into our hearts through the Holy Spirit.

PART I

Introduction to Sacramental Theology

This book is an introduction to the sacraments of healing—Penance and Anointing of the Sick. However, before looking in detail at these two sacraments, we will first consider the nature and power of the sacraments in general. The first three chapters of this volume present a concise introduction to sacramental theology: What is a sacrament? How does God act through the sacraments? How do the sacraments affect our lives? How can we enter more fully into each sacramental celebration?

The *Catechism of the Catholic Church* describes a sacramental celebration as "a meeting of God's children with their Father, in Christ and the Holy Spirit" (CCC, 1153). This is the fundamental conviction of this book: the sacraments are encounters with the Father in Christ and the Holy Spirit—the Trinity. We will begin by examining in chapter 1 how the sacraments fulfill Christ's promise to his apostles to be with them always. We will look particularly at how each person of the Trinity—Father, Son, and Holy Spirit—is present and active in a sacramental celebration. We will give special attention to how the sacraments make present the Passion, Death, Resurrection, and Ascension of Christ and how they dispense divine life to us (CCC, 1131).

The focus of chapter 2 is on the meeting of God with his children in a sacramental celebration that "takes the form of a dialogue, through actions and words," that is, through signs that comprise a sacramental language (CCC, 1153). Here we will look at several signs which are common to many or all of the sacraments: signs such as images, song, the Sign of the Cross, movement, incense, and color. Our discussion of these different sacramental signs will focus on how they are "bearers of the saving and sanctifying action of Christ," how the Spirit acts through these signs to impart to us the power of Christ's saving sacrifice to the praise and glory of God the Father (CCC, 1189).

In order for us to participate fully and fruitfully in sacramental celebrations, we must approach them with faith and understanding. The final chapter of this section describes an approach to liturgical catechesis that helps us do that. It has three elements. It begins by looking at the Old Testament roots of the sacrament, revealing the unity and progressive fulfillment of God's saving work that culminates in the person and work of Jesus Christ. Next, it analyzes the meaning of the different liturgical signs that comprise each sacrament. Finally, it considers the way each sacrament transforms our lives. In chapter 3 we will describe this method of catechesis and illustrate it with examples from the sacraments of initiation (Baptism, Eucharist, and Confirmation) and the sacraments of vocation (Holy Orders and Matrimony). Taken together, these first three chapters will give us the foundation and tools for a detailed study of the Sacraments of Penance and the Anointing of the Sick.

Chapter 1

The Sacraments: An Encounter with the Blessed Trinity

As Jesus was about to ascend to the Father, he gathered his disciples on the mountain. There he commanded them to "make disciples of all nations" and promised to be with them always: "And behold, I am with you always, until the end of the age" (Mt 28:19–20). Then "he parted from them and was taken up to heaven" (Lk 24:51). Luke tells us that the disciples experienced the Ascension with joy, not sadness: "they did him homage and then returned to Jerusalem with great joy" (Lk 24:52).

Why were the disciples joyful at Jesus departure? Because they had experienced Christ's new way of being with them. His sacramental presence is beautifully expressed in his encounter with the two disciples on the road to Emmaus who do not recognize him (Lk 24:13–35). After an introductory conversation (vv.13–24), "beginning with Moses and all the prophets, [Jesus] interpreted to them what referred to him in all the scriptures" (v. 27). The two disciples then invited him to stay with them, and they shared a meal. When Jesus was at table with them, "he took bread, said the blessing, broke it, and gave it to them" (v. 30)—taking, blessing, breaking and giving are Eucharistic actions. "With that their eyes were opened and they recognized him, but he vanished from their sight" (v. 31).

This account has the same structure as the Mass. It begins with the Liturgy of the Word—Jesus explaining to them how the Scriptures speak of him—and it culminates with the Liturgy of the Eucharist, when Jesus took bread, blessed it, broke it, and gave it to them. At that moment he vanished from their sight, because he was now present in the Eucharist. This is Luke's way of explaining Jesus' new way of being with his disciples—his presence is now a sacramental presence, manifested through sacramental signs, preeminently through the signs of bread and wine. "In this age of the Church Christ now lives and acts in and with his Church, in a new way appropriate to this new age" (CCC, 1076). Christ the Head is now present in and acts powerfully through

9

his Body the Church, which "is like a sacrament (sign and instrument) in which the Holy Spirit dispenses the mystery of salvation" (CCC, 1111). Christ continues to proclaim the Kingdom of God through words and deeds, just as he did during his earthly ministry, only the manner is different—bodily in the Gospels, now sacramentally through signs and symbols, words and actions, through his Body, the Church, in the liturgy. The *Catechism* explains how Christ acts through the sacraments by recalling healing miracles found in the Gospel according to Luke in which power came forth from Jesus to heal the sick. On one occasion, for example, a crowd was trying to touch Jesus, "because power came forth from him and healed them all" (Lk 6:19). On another occasion, a woman who had been sick for twelve years touched the fringe of his garment and was healed. Jesus instantly knew what had happened. He told Peter, "Someone has touched me; for I know that *power has gone out from me*" (8:46; italics added). These events prefigure what Christ now accomplishes through the sacraments: "Sacraments are '*powers that come forth'* from the Body of Christ, which is ever-living and life-giving" (CCC, 1116; italics added). All that Jesus did during his earthly ministry he continues to do today through the sacraments—*sacramentally*—"by means of signs perceptible to the senses" (SC, 7).

THE PASCHAL MYSTERY

There is a second reason why the disciples were joyful at his Ascension. Jesus was still with them and he had introduced a new presence and power into the world through his Paschal Mystery. Christ's Paschal Mystery (from the Greek noun *pascha*, which means "Passover," and the Greek verb *paschō*, which means "to suffer") refers to "his blessed passion, resurrection from the dead, and glorious ascension, whereby 'dying, he destroyed our death, and rising, restored our life'" (SC, 5). The Paschal Mystery is unique among all historical events: while all other historical events happen and then pass away, the Paschal Mystery "cannot remain only in the past, because by his death he destroyed death, and all that Christ is—all that he did and suffered for all men—participates in the divine eternity, and so transcends all times while being made present in them all. The event of the Cross and Resurrection *abides* and draws everything toward life" (CCC, 1085). It is not just an event which we reverently remember, it is an ever-present reality "that the Church proclaims and celebrates in her liturgy so that the faithful may live from it and bear witness to it in the world" (CCC, 1068). It constitutes, wrote St. John Paul II, "the content of the daily life of the Church" (VQA, 6).

There is an integral connection between Jesus' earthly ministry and his Paschal Mystery. His words and actions during his earthly ministry anticipated in different ways the saving power of the Paschal Mystery that is now communicated through the Church in the liturgy (CCC, 1085). He himself was baptized by John in the Jordan, and he commanded his disciples to baptize new believers; he commissioned and empowered his followers to continue this ministry (Mt 28:18–20). He healed the sick and sent his disciples out to do the same (Mt 10:1). He forgave sinners and imparted the Spirit to the Apostles to continue this ministry (cf. Jn 20:22–23). He celebrated the Last Supper with his disciples and commanded them to celebrate it often (Mt 26:26–29). He imparted to the Twelve a special power and authority to act in his name, and the Apostles continued this in the early Church (Lk 24:49). In these events Christ announced and prepared what he would give the Church when all had been accomplished (Jn 19:30). "The mysteries of Christ's life are the foundations of what he would henceforth dispense in the sacraments, through the ministers of his Church" (CCC, 1115). In the memorable formulation of Pope St. Leo the Great (d. 461), "what was visible in our Savior has passed over into his mysteries [sacraments]" (CCC, 1115).

THE PASCHAL MYSTERY AND THE OTHER SACRAMENTS

All of the sacraments draw their power from the Paschal Mystery of Christ. "The Paschal Mystery is celebrated and made present in the liturgy of the Church, and its saving effects are communicated through the sacraments" (CCC, glossary). This is true in a preeminent way of the Eucharist, for "in the sacrifice of the Mass the passion of Christ is again made present" (RP, 2). However, it is also true of the other sacraments. For example, the *Rite of Baptism* explains the effects of Baptism: it is "the door to life and to the kingdom of God" (GICI, 3); it incorporates recipients into the Church (GICI, 4); and it "washes away every stain of sin, original and personal, makes us sharers in God's own life and his adopted children" (GICI, 5). All of these effects are produced "by the power of the mystery of the Lord's passion and resurrection. . . . For baptism recalls and makes present the paschal mystery itself, because in baptism we pass from the death of sin into life" (GICI, 6).

The Sacrament of Marriage also derives its power from the Paschal Mystery, as we hear in one of the prefaces: "as you have redeemed man and woman by the mystery of Christ's Death and Resurrection, so in Christ you might make them partakers of divine nature and joint heirs with him of heavenly glory. In the union of husband and wife, you give a sign of Christ's loving gift of grace, so that the Sacrament we celebrate might draw us back more deeply into the wondrous design of your love" (RM, Ritual Mass for the Celebration of Marriage, Preface B). The *Catechism* summarizes the relationship between the Paschal Mystery and the sacraments as follows: "The Paschal Mystery is celebrated and made present in the liturgy of the Church, and its saving effects are communicated through the sacraments, especially the Eucharist, which renews the paschal sacrifice of Christ as the sacrifice offered by the Church" (CCC, glossary).

THE SACRAMENTS: THE WORK OF THE TRINITY

While Christ's role in the liturgy is rightly emphasized, it is important to remember that the Paschal Mystery is the work of the entire Trinity, as we read in the Letter to the Hebrews: "*Christ*, who through the eternal *spirit*, offered himself without blemish to *God*" (9:14; italics added). Indeed, everything accomplished by God in creation and salvation history is the joint work of the Trinity.[1] This is how St. Teresa of Avila explained it: "In all three Persons there is no more than one will, one power, and one dominion, in such a way that one cannot do anything without the others. . . . Could the Son create an ant without the Father? No, for it is all one power, and the same goes for the Holy Spirit; thus there is only one all-powerful God and all three Persons are one Majesty."[2]

---

1. "However, each divine person performs the common work according to his unique personal property" (CCC, 258).

2. Teresa of Avila, *The Collected Works of Teresa of Avila*, trans. Kieran Kavanagh, OCD, and Otilio Rodriguez, OCD, vol. 1, *The Book of Her Life, Spiritual Testimonies, Soliloquies* (Washington, DC: ICS Publications, 1976), 401.

The sacraments are the work of the Trinity, for "a sacramental celebration is a meeting of God's children with their Father, in Christ and the Holy Spirit" (CCC, 1153). The Father is the source of blessing, which "is a divine and life-giving action" (CCC, 1078). "From the beginning until the end of time the whole of God's work is a *blessing*" (CCC, 1079). Examples of God's blessing include creation, his covenants with Noah and Abraham, the deliverance from Egypt, the gift of the promised land, God's presence in the Temple, and Israel's purifying exile and return (CCC, 1080–1081). However, it is in the liturgy that "the divine blessing is fully revealed and communicated" (CCC, 1082). Since the liturgy is a dialogue, we respond to the revelation and communication of the Father's blessing by rendering to him blessing and adoration for "all the blessings of creation and salvation with which he has blessed us in his Son, in order to give us the Spirit of filial adoption" (CCC, 1110).

Christ's action in the liturgy is to point to and make present through perceptible signs—his new, sacramental way of being with us—his own Paschal Mystery. He accomplishes this by manifesting his sacramental presence in a number of ways. He is present in the assembly in fulfillment of his promise that "where two or three are gathered together in my name, there am I in the midst of them" (Mt 18:20). He is present in his ordained ministers, who are "sacramental signs of Christ" (CCC, 1087). He is present in his Word. And he is present "especially under the eucharistic elements" (SC, 7). Christ acts in the liturgy according to his new way of being with us, communicating to us the fruits of his Passion, Death, Resurrection, and Ascension.

The Holy Spirit, "teacher of the faith of the People of God and artisan of 'God's masterpieces,' the sacraments of the New Covenant" (CCC, 1091), acts in a number of ways in the liturgy. He prepares the people of God to receive Christ by awakening faith, conversion of heart, and adherence to the Father's will (CCC, 1098). He also recalls the mystery of Christ by "giving life to the Word of God," giving "a spiritual understanding of the Word of God," and "gives the grace of faith" to the listeners so that they may respond to the word in faith (CCC, 1100–1102). The Spirit also makes present the Paschal Mystery of Christ through his "transforming power in the liturgy (CCC, 1107). Finally, the Holy Spirit, "who is the Spirit of communion," brings the assembly into communion with Christ, forming them into his Body (CCC, 1108). The section of the *Catechism* on the Holy Spirit

(1091–1109) in the liturgy is worth a careful and prayerful reading, for it "makes a remarkable contribution to a new Trinitarian understanding of the liturgy."[3]

The presence and work of the Trinity is clearly expressed in Eucharistic Prayer III: "You are indeed Holy, O *Lord* . . . for through your Son our Lord *Jesus Christ,* by the power and working of the *Holy Spirit,* you give life to all things and make them holy" (italics added). God the Father, through the Son, by the power and working of the Holy Spirit, gives life and sanctifies all things. The Sacrament of Baptism is also an encounter with the Trinity, for "the blessed Trinity is invoked over those who are to be baptized, so that all who are signed in this name are consecrated to the Trinity and enter into communion with the Father, the Son, and the Holy Spirit" (*Rite of Baptism for Children,* Christian Initiation, General Introduction, 7). Thus, every sacramental celebration is an action of the three Persons of the Trinity and draws us ever more deeply into the mystery of Trinitarian love.

THE NATURE OF THE LITURGY

Before considering in more detail the sacraments as works of the Trinity, we need to look briefly at the nature of the liturgy. In the *Constitution on the Sacred Liturgy* the Second Vatican Council described the liturgy in the following terms:

> Rightly, then, the liturgy is considered as an exercise of the priestly office of Jesus Christ. In the liturgy, by means of signs perceptible to the senses, human sanctification is signified and brought about in ways proper to each of these signs; in the liturgy the whole public worship is performed by the Mystical Body of Jesus Christ, that is, by the Head and his members.
>
> From this it follows that every liturgical celebration, because it is an action of Christ the Priest and of his Body which is the Church, is a sacred action surpassing all others; no other action of the Church can equal its effectiveness by the same title and to the same degree. (SC, 7)

---

3. Francis Eugene Cardinal George, OMI, "*Sacrosanctum Concilium* Anniversary Address: The Foundations of Liturgical Reform," in *Cardinal Reflections: Active Participation and the Liturgy* (Chicago: Hillenbrand Books, 2005), 47.

This description makes three important assertions.

- First, the liturgy is "an exercise of the priestly office of Jesus Christ," which means that he is the celebrant at every liturgy.
- Second, Christ is present in the liturgy through "signs perceptible to the sense" and he works "in ways proper to each of these signs." This is what we mean when we speak of Christ being present and acting *sacramentally*—he is truly present, but now through "signs perceptible to the senses."
- Third, the liturgy "is performed by the Mystical Body of Jesus Christ, that is, by the Head and his members." Christ is manifested sacramentally as Body and Head in distinct ways.

CHRIST IS PRESENT, HEAD AND BODY

Christ's presence in his Mystical Body is a fulfillment of his promise to his disciples: "Where two or three are gathered together in my name, there am I in the midst of them" (Mt 18:20). Although this presence is manifested in different ways, we will look at only one example. In the Eucharist it is accomplished through the celebrant's Greeting—"The Lord be with you"—and the people's response—"And with your spirit." The celebrant's greeting "signifies the presence of the Lord to the assembled community" (GIRM, 50). Together with the people's response, "the mystery of the Church gathered together is made manifest" (GIRM, 50). In other words, through this simple dialogue, a profound change takes place—the congregation has become a new sacramental reality—it has become the Mystical Body of Christ gathered in this place, making visibly present the mystery of the Church. It is no longer just a group of people gathered in one place; now it is the Body of Christ prepared to perform the public worship of the Church.

The greeting and response also make sacramentally present Christ the Head. According to the *Catechism of the Catholic Church*, "Through the ordained ministry, especially that of bishops and priests, the presence of Christ as head of the Church is made visible in the midst of the community" (CCC, 1549). In the Eucharist, this visible presence of Christ as head is manifested especially through the people's response, "And with your spirit." This is more than a simple greeting along the lines of "and also with you"; it is a reference to the gift of the Spirit received at ordination. This understanding of the people's response is very ancient. In the fifth century, Narsai of Nisibis explained that "spirit" refers "not to the soul of the priest but to the Spirit he has received through the laying on of hands."[4] It is only through the gift of the Spirit received at ordination that the liturgy is able to go forward. In the words of a contemporary scholar, "The community's response could be understood as a short intercession for its president, that he may fulfill well his role as president with the help of the Lord and in the ministerial grace bestowed by his Spirit."[5] The Church also urges the priest to make this sacramental reality apparent through his celebration of the Mass: "by his bearing and by the way he pronounces the divine words he must convey to the faithful the living presence of Christ" (GIRM, 93).

THE WORD OF GOD

Christ is present through his Word in multiple ways in the liturgy. First, "it is from Scripture that the readings are given and explained in the homily and that psalms are sung" (SC, 24), for when the Holy Scriptures are proclaimed in the liturgy, it is "he himself who speaks" (SC, 7). Second, "the prayers, collects, and liturgical songs are *scriptural in their inspiration*" (italics added). Third, "it is from the Scriptures that actions and signs derive their meaning" (SC, 24). Christ the eternal Word proclaims his Word in the liturgical assembly, his Word gives the prayers and liturgical text their unique power, and it interprets the signs and actions that comprise the liturgy.

Indeed, there is an intrinsic unity between God's deeds and words. "In salvation history there is no separation between what God *says* and what he *does*. His word appears as alive and active (cf. Heb 4:12)" (VD, 53). God created through his word: "God said: Let there be light, and there was light" (Gen 1:3). This same power is evident in many of Jesus' miracles. Jesus said to the paralytic, "I say to you, rise, pick up your mat, and go home" (Mk 2:11), and he was immediately healed. When Jesus and his disciples were engulfed in a storm at sea,

---

4. Robert Cabie, *The Eucharist*, trans. Matthew J. O'Connell, in *The Church at Prayer*, vol. 2 (Collegeville, MN: The Liturgical Press, 1986), 51.

5. Michael Kunzler, *The Church's Liturgy*, trans. Placed Murray, OSB, Henry O'Shea, OSB, and Cilian Ó Sé, OSB (London: Continuum, 2001), 198.

Jesus rebuked the wind and said to the sea, "Quiet! Be still!"(Mk 4:39). The wind immediately ceased and a great calm prevailed. Pope Benedict XVI calls this the "performative character" of God's word, which is not confined to the past, but is a present reality. "In the liturgical action too, we encounter his word which accomplishes what it says" (VD, 53).

The performative character of the Word of Christ in the liturgy is supremely evident in the Eucharist when the priest pronounces the words of Christ over the bread and wine. This is how St. John Chrysostom (d. 407) explained this mystery: "The priest, in the role of Christ, pronounces these words, but their power and grace are God's. This is my body, he says. This word transforms the things offered" (CCC, 1375).[6] Sixteen hundred years later, St. John Paul II affirmed this same reality. It is the priest "who says with the power coming to him from Christ in the Upper Room: 'This is my body which will be given up for you. . . . This is the cup of my blood, poured out for you . . . ' The priest says these words, or rather *he puts his voice at the disposal of the One who spoke these words in the Upper Room* . . . " (EE, 5). God's Word is efficacious, accomplishing what it signifies.

The Word of God proclaimed in the liturgy "is always a living and effective word through the power of the Holy Spirit. It expresses the Father's love that never fails in its effectiveness towards us" (VD, 52). The Word of the Father is made present and personal through the action of the Holy Spirit. "In the word of God proclaimed and heard, and in the sacraments, Jesus says today, here and now, to each person: 'I am yours, I give myself to you'; so that we can receive and respond, saying in return: 'I am yours'" (VD, 51). Understanding the performative character of God's Word in the liturgy can help us recognize God's activity in salvation history and in our own lives (VD, 53), acting at times in ways that surprise and amaze us, for as Pope Francis reminds us, "God's word is unpredictable in its power." (EG, 22).

---

6. It is the constant teaching of the Church that the bread and wine are transformed into the Body and Blood of Christ *through the Word of Christ and the working of the Holy Spirit*: "The Church Fathers strongly affirmed the faith of the Church in the efficacy of the Word of Christ and of the action of the Holy Spirit to bring about this conversion" (CCC, 1375).

Digging into the Catechism

The reading of the Gospel during Mass is accompanied by a rich variety of sacramental signs. What are the different signs that accompany this key moment of the Mass? (Cf. CCC, 1154)

INVOKING THE HOLY SPIRIT: THE EPICLESIS

One of the essential elements in every sacramental celebration is the invocation of the Holy Spirit. This invocation is called the *epiclesis*, from the Greek word meaning "to call upon." Every sacrament includes an epiclesis, a "prayer asking for the sanctifying power of God's Holy Spirit" (CCC, glossary). It is accompanied by a gesture dating back to the Apostles: "The life-giving power of the Spirit, who moved over the waters in the first days of creation and overshadowed Mary in the moment of the incarnation, is vividly expressed by the ancient gesture of bringing together the hands with the palms downward and extended over the elements to be consecrated" (IOM, 118).

Let's look at a few examples. In the Sacrament of Baptism there is an epiclesis on the baptismal water. This epiclesis reads as follows:

> May the power of the Holy Spirit,
> O Lord, we pray,
> come down through your Son
> into the fullness of this font,
> so that all who have been buried with Christ
> by Baptism into death
> may rise again to life with him
> (RM, Easter Vigil, Blessing of Baptismal Water, n. 44).

In the Mass we find two epicleses. The first, spoken over the bread and wine to change them into the Body and Blood of Christ, is called the consecratory epiclesis. The second epiclesis, invoked over the congregation, is called the communion epiclesis, because it asks "that those who take part in the Eucharist may be one body and one spirit" (CCC, 1353). The epiclesis is an essential element of every liturgical celebration, ensuring that "there is an outpouring of the Holy Spirit that makes the unique mystery present" (CCC, 1104).

LITURGICAL REMEMBERING: THE ANAMNESIS

The second element "at the heart of each sacramental celebration" (CCC, 1106) is the anamnesis. The word itself is a transliteration of a Greek word that is translated as "reminder" or "remembrance." It occurs twice in the earliest account of the Last Supper, 1 Corinthians 11:23–26, written by St. Paul in the mid-50s. Jesus' words over the bread (11:24) and the cup (11:25) conclude with the command to "do this . . . in remembrance [anamnesis] of me." The anamnesis, the "remembrance" or "memorial," is "a living re-presentation before God of the saving deeds he has accomplished in Christ, so that their fullness and power may be effective here and now" (IOM, 121).

The anamnesis or remembrance "is not merely the recollection of past events but the proclamation of the mighty works wrought by God for men. In the liturgical celebration of these events, *they become in a certain way present and real*. This is how Israel understands its liberation from Egypt: every time Passover is celebrated, the Exodus events are made present to the memory of believers so that they may conform their lives to them" (CCC, 1363; italics added). "In the New Testament, the memorial takes on new meaning. When the Church celebrates the Eucharist, she commemorates Christ's Passover, and *it is made present*: the sacrifice Christ offered once for all on the cross remains ever present. 'As often as the sacrifice of the Cross by which "Christ our Pasch has been sacrificed" is celebrated on the altar, the work of our redemption is carried out'" (CCC, 1364; italics added).

In the Rite of Baptism the anamnesis is found in the Prayer over the Water: "O God, whose Son, / baptized by John in the waters of the Jordan, / was anointed with the Holy Spirit, / and, *as he hung upon the Cross, gave forth water from his side along with blood, / and after his Resurrection,* commanded his disciples: / 'Go forth, teach all nations, / baptizing them / in the name of the Father and of the Son and of the Holy Spirit.'" (RM, Easter Vigil, Blessing of Baptismal Water, n. 46; italics added). In the Mass, every Eucharistic Prayer contains an anamnesis "in which the Church calls to mind the Passion, Resurrection, and glorious return of Christ Jesus" (CCC, glossary). The anamnesis always comes after the words of institution and is followed by the oblation, in which the Church "presents to the Father the offering of his Son which reconciles us with him" (CCC, 1354). In Eucharistic Prayer III the anamnesis, offering, and thanksgiving or doxology are expressed eloquently and concisely: "Therefore, O Lord, as we celebrate the memorial of the saving Passion of your Son, his wondrous Resurrection and Ascension into heaven, and as we look forward to his second coming [anamnesis], we offer you [offering] in thanksgiving [doxology] this holy and living sacrifice."

THE REAL PRESENCE—PAR EXCELLENCE

Finally, Christ is present in the Eucharistic species in a manner that is utterly unique and "raises the Eucharist above all the sacraments as 'the perfection of the spiritual life and the end to which all the sacraments tend'" (CCC, 1374). In the Eucharistic species "the body and blood, together with the soul and divinity, of our Lord Jesus Christ and, therefore, *the whole Christ is truly, really, and substantially* contained" (CCC, 1374): truly, "not simply through image or form," really, "not only subjectively through the faith of believers," and substantially, "in his profound reality, which cannot be seen by the senses, and not in the appearances which remain that of bread and wine."[7] In affirming the real presence of Christ in the Eucharistic species the Church is not denying Christ's real presence in other ways, such as in his word and in the assembly gathered in his name. Rather, his presence in the Eucharistic species "is presence in the fullest sense: that is to say, it is a *substantial* presence by which Christ, God and man, makes himself wholly and entirely present" (CCC, 1374). The Eucharist, therefore, contains "the entire spiritual wealth of the church, namely Christ himself our Pasch" (PO, 5).

This presence is expressed in several ways in the words of the Mass. In the Liturgy of the Eucharist, the Preface, Eucharistic Prayer, and Our Father are all addressed to God the Father. However, the prayers following the Our Father are addressed to Christ, now substantially present on the altar: "Lord Jesus Christ, who said to your apostles . . . ," and "Lamb of God, you take away the sins of the world, have mercy on us." Finally, the priest shows the consecrated host and blood and says, "Behold the Lamb of God, behold him who takes away the sins of the world" (IOM, 132). We do not behold "It", a holy thing, but the person of Christ, the Son of

---

7. Raniero Cantalamessa, *The Eucharist: Our Sanctification*, rev. ed. (Collegeville, MN: The Liturgical Press, 1995), 81.

God, under the appearance of bread. Sacramental communion also has the character of a personal encounter. For this reason, "ordained ministers and those who . . . are authorized to exercise the ministry of distributing the Eucharist [should] make every effort to ensure that this simple act preserves its importance as a personal encounter with the Lord Jesus in the sacrament" (SacCar, 50).

St. Teresa of Avila expressed the reality of Christ's presence in the Eucharist with particularly vivid and personal language: "Receiving Communion is not like picturing with the imagination. . . . In Communion the event is happening now, and it is entirely true. . . . Now, then, if when He went about in the world the mere touch of His robes cured the sick, why doubt, if we have faith, that miracles will be worked while He is within us and that He will give what we ask of Him, since He is in our house? His Majesty is not accustomed to paying poorly for His lodging if the hospitality is good."[8]

Finally, the presence of Christ in the liturgy is manifested through the signs and symbols which make up the liturgical rites. Through the power of the Spirit, they "become *bearers of the saving and sanctifying action of Christ*" (CCC, 1189; italics added). They comprise the language of the liturgy, which is the subject of the next chapter.

---

8. Teresa of Avila, *The Collected Works of Teresa of Avila*, trans. Kieran Kavanaugh, OCD, and Otilio Rodriguez, OCD, vol. 2, *The Way of Perfection, Meditations on the Song of Sons, The Interior Castle* (Washington, DC: ICS Publications, 1980), 172.

Chapter 2

The Language of the Liturgy

The liturgy is composed of signs and symbols through which God manifests his presence as well as his saving and sanctifying action. He mediates his presence through signs and symbols because this corresponds to our very nature, to the way he created us. We are both body and spirit, so we express and perceive "spiritual realities through physical signs and symbols" (CCC, 1146). In addition, because we have been created as social beings, we need "signs and symbols to communicate with others, through language, gestures, and actions" (CCC, 1146). This is equally true of our relationship with God. "For in God's design the humanity and loving kindness of our Savior have visibly appeared to us and so God uses visible signs to give salvation and to renew the broken covenant" (RP, 6d).

The signs of the liturgy confer salvation and renew the broken covenant because they are "bearers of the saving and sanctifying action of Christ" (CCC, 1189). Their power stems from their origin: "the visible signs used by the liturgy to signify invisible divine things have been chosen by Christ or the Church" (SC, 33). Examples of signs chosen by Christ include unleavened bread and grape wine for the Eucharist, the use of oil for the anointing of the sick, and the baptismal formula "in the name of the Father and of the Son and of the Holy Spirit." Signs chosen by the Church include liturgical vestments and colors, postures such as standing and kneeling, and gestures such as the sign of the cross. These signs, whether chosen by Christ or the Church, are bearers of the power of Christ's Paschal Mystery in a way that is not possible with signs chosen by us. Furthermore, they are "necessary for the mystery of salvation to be really effective in the Christian community" and to ensure "the presence of God."(LI, 1). Through signs the liturgy makes present the transforming power of Christ's Paschal Mystery, bringing us into relationship with the Trinity.

When the Church speaks of liturgical signs, she uses the term in a broad and comprehensive way, including material objects, words, actions, song and music. They are drawn from elements and actions "relating to creation (candles, water, fire), human life (washing, anointing, breaking bread) and the history of salvation (the rites of the Passover)" (CCC, 1189). All of the liturgical signs and symbols are related to Christ and find their fulfillment in him. When we talk about liturgical signs and symbols, the distinction between sign and symbol is not the important point: "what is important is that, whichever term is employed—be it 'sign' or 'symbol'—the meaning each has for the Church is one of fullness, reality, and truth. In fact, that to which signs and symbols point is *the* fullness, reality, and truth: Christ himself."[1] The Trinity acts through the liturgical signs: the Holy Spirit uses the words, actions and signs that make up a liturgical celebration to put "both the faithful and the ministers into a living relationship with Christ, the Word and Image of the Father, so that they can live out the meaning of what they hear, contemplate, and do in the celebration" (CCC, 1101). Through the faith of the Church and the power of the Holy Spirit, God communicates the fruits of Christ's Paschal Mystery to us by means of this liturgical language.

There is a close relationship between the power of liturgical signs and their intelligibility. The intelligibility of the signs and symbols of the liturgy was a primary concern of the Second Vatican Council in its reform of the liturgy. "It is, therefore, of the greatest importance that the faithful should easily understand the sacramental signs" (SC, 59) so that they can "take part in them fully, actively, and as a community" (SC, 21). Intelligible signs enable the liturgy to enter "firmly and effectively . . . into the minds and lives of the faithful" (EM, 4). When misunderstood, the language of the liturgy can be confusing or meaningless, but when understood it is inexhaustibly rich, varied and powerful.

SACRAMENTAL SIGNS AND SYMBOLS

Sacramental signs are different from the signs that we encounter in our daily life. For example, a hospital sign indicates the location of a hospital, but it does not contain the hospital itself. It is merely an indicator, a pointer. Sacramental signs also point to another reality, but unlike conventional signs, they also *make present* the reality they signify. "The

---

1. Christopher Carstens and Douglas Martis, *Mystical Body, Mystical Voice: Encountering Christ in the Words of the Mass* (Chicago: Liturgy Training Publications, 2011), 40.

liturgical word and action are inseparable both insofar as they are signs and instruction and insofar as *they accomplish what they signify*. When the Holy Spirit awakens faith, he not only gives an understanding of the Word of God, but *through the sacraments also makes present the 'wonders' of God* which it proclaims" (CCC, 1155; italics added). This reality is expressed in the liturgy itself. Consider, for example, the Prayer after Communion for the Thirtieth Sunday in Ordinary Time:

> May your Sacraments, O Lord, we pray,
> perfect in us what lies within them,
> that what we now celebrate in signs
> we may one day possess in truth.

God uses the signs and symbols of the liturgy to communicate the power and reality of the Paschal Mystery to us.

Through the richness and diversity of its signs, the liturgy engages the whole person: mind, body and senses. It engages the hearing through words and song; smell through incense; sight through vestments, images, colors; feeling through posture and gesture; and taste through the Body and Blood of Christ under the appearance of bread and wine. Through these different "kinds of language" the liturgy operates "on different levels of communication" and engages the whole person (SacCar, 40) so that each participant can enter into the liturgy with his or her whole being.

Let us now consider some of the signs common to all of the sacraments. We looked at a few liturgical signs in the previous chapter, such as the liturgical word and the gesture that accompanies the invocation of the Holy Spirit. In this chapter we will consider additional signs and symbols that are common to many of the Church's sacramental celebrations: images, song, the sign of the cross, silence, movement, incense, and color. Finally, we will consider the importance of the harmony of the liturgical signs.

Images

An element common to all Catholic churches, and therefore a part of every liturgical celebration, is the liturgical image. Sacred art is a direct consequence of the Incarnation. No image can "represent the invisible and incomprehensible God, but the incarnation of the Son of God has ushered in a new 'economy' of images" (CCC, 1159). St. John Damascene explained this new "economy of images" in the seventh century: "Previously God, who has neither a body nor a face, absolutely could not be represented by an image. But now that he has made himself visible in the flesh and has lived with men, I can make an image of what I have seen of God . . . and contemplate the glory of the Lord, his face unveiled" (CCC, 1159). The sacred image and sacred word teach and reinforce the one Gospel message of Jesus Christ. In 787, the Second Council of Nicaea affirmed this reciprocal relationship between Sacred Scripture and sacred art: "the production of representational artwork . . . accords with the history of the preaching of the Gospel. For it confirms that the incarnation of the Word of God was real and not imaginary, and to our benefit as well, for realities that illustrate each other undoubtedly reflect each other's meaning" (CCC, 1160).

Sacred images "truly signify Christ, who is glorified in them" (CCC, 1161), and in a certain way make present an integral aspect of every sacramental celebration, the "cloud of witnesses" spoken of in Hebrews 12:1, "who continue to participate in the salvation of the world and to whom we are united, above all in sacramental celebrations" (CCC, 1161). This heavenly dimension was reaffirmed by the Second Vatican Council: "In the earthly liturgy we take part in a foretaste of that heavenly liturgy which is celebrated in the holy city of Jerusalem toward which we journey as pilgrims, where Christ is sitting at the right hand of God, a minister of the holies and of the true tabernacle; we sing a hymn to the Lord's glory with all the warriors of the heavenly army" (SC, 8). Sacramental celebrations unite heaven and earth, joining us with the entire heavenly host, as evidenced, for example, in the invocation of the Penitential Rite:

> . . . therefore I ask Blessed Mary ever-Virgin,
> all the Angels and Saints,
> and you, my brothers and sisters
> to pray for me to the Lord our God.
> (RM, Order of Mass, Penitential Act)

This heavenly, vertical dimension of the liturgy is deeply rooted in our tradition. In the fifth century St. John Chrysostom described the angelic presence at the Eucharist: "The angels surround the priest. The whole sanctuary and the space around the altar are filled with the heavenly powers to honor him who is present on the altar."[2] Three centuries later St. Bede (d. 735) exhorted the faithful in the following words: "We are not permitted to doubt that where the mysteries of the Lord's body and blood are being enacted, a gathering of the citizens from on high is present. . . . Hence we must strive meticulously, my brothers, when we come into the church to pay the due service of divine praise or to perform the solemnity of the mass, to be always mindful of the angelic presence, and to fulfill our heavenly duty with fear and fitting veneration."[3] In a real and powerful way heaven becomes present on earth at every liturgical celebration.

Sacred images are an integral part of the liturgy, for they help us perceive the heavenly host present with us at every liturgical celebration. "Images point to a presence; they are essentially connected with what happens in the liturgy. Their whole point is to lead us beyond what can be apprehended at the merely material level, to awaken new senses in us, and to teach us *a new kind of seeing*, which perceives the Invisible in the visible."[4] Sacred images help us to "look not to the things that are seen but to the things that are unseen; for the things that are seen are transient, but the things that are unseen are eternal" (2 Cor 4:18). Every liturgical celebration is a participation in the heavenly liturgy eternally celebrated in the heavenly Jerusalem. Sacred images assist us in understanding and entering into this vital aspect of the liturgy.

Song

Music, as with all liturgical signs, manifests the presence of God, for "God, the giver of song, is present whenever his people sing his praises" (SL, 1). It enriches the liturgy in a variety of ways. Prayer, when sung, "is expressed in a more attractive way" (SL, 1). Song also manifests more clearly the "hierarchical and communal nature" of "the mystery of the liturgy", since different parts of the liturgy are sung by the priest celebrant (the prayers/orations, the preface), the cantor (the responsorial psalm), the schola or choir, and the entire assembly (e.g., the Kyrie, the

---

2. Jean Daniélou, SJ, *The Angels and Their Mission*, trans. David Heimann (Westminster, MD: The Newman press, 1956), 62.

3. Erik M. Heen and Philip D.W. Krey, eds., *Hebrews*, Ancient Christian Commentary on Scripture (Downers Grove, IL: InterVarsity Press, 2005), 30.

4. Joseph Ratzinger, *The Spirit of the Liturgy*, trans. John Saward (San Francisco: Ignatius, 2000), 133; italics added.

Gloria, and the Entrance chant) (SL, 10). The union of voices contributes "to the unity of hearts" (MS, 5), one of the ways that we, though many, are one body in Christ. Also, through song "minds are more easily raised to heavenly things by the beauty of the sacred rites" (MS, 5). St. John Chrysostom emphasized this dimension in the exhortation "Lift up your hearts": "Let no one have any thought of earthy, but let him lose himself of every earthly thing and transport himself whole and entire into heaven. Let him abide there beside the very throne of glory, hovering with the Seraphim, and singing the most holy song of the God of glory and majesty."[5]

As we noted above, the earthly liturgy is a participation in the heavenly liturgy. Music is an important aspect of that participation. In the words of the Second Vatican Council, "we sing a hymn to the Lord's glory with all the warriors of the heavenly army" (SC, 8). St. John Chrysostom described this dimension of the liturgy: "Think now of what kind of choir you are going to enter. Although vested with a body, you have been judged worthy to join the Powers of heaven in singing the praises of Him who is Lord of all."[6] Music and song, along with sacred images, manifest the heavenly dimension of the earthly liturgy. Through song, the whole liturgy "more clearly prefigures that heavenly liturgy which is enacted in the holy city of Jerusalem" (MS, 5).

Music in the liturgy is a rich and powerful bearer of the saving and sanctifying power of Christ in many ways. It enhances prayer. It manifests the mystery of the Church, which is simultaneously hierarchical and unified. It helps us set our mind on heavenly things. Through song we join the heavenly choir that never ceases to sing the praises of God (Rev 4:8). Liturgical song is "a sign of God's love for us and of our love for him" (SL, 2), one of the sacramental signs through which we are brought into unity with the Trinity and with one another, are made holy, and give glory to God.

The Sign of the Cross

Gestures are another kind of liturgical sign. Perhaps the one that is most common and familiar to every sacramental celebration is the sign of the cross. This is a very ancient Christian gesture. Tertullian (ca. 220) saw

---

5. Daniélou, *Angels,* 62.

6. Ibid.

the sign of the cross prefigured in Ezekiel 9:4, in which the Lord instructed the prophet to go through Jerusalem and mark on the forehead those "who sigh and groan over all the abominations that are committed in it." Here is Tertullian's explanation:

> [Christ] foretold that His just ones should suffer equally with Him—both the apostles and all the faithful in succession; and He signed them with that very seal of which Ezekiel spake: "The Lord said unto me, go through the gate, through the midst of Jerusalem, and set the mark *Tau* upon the foreheads of the men." Now the Greek letter *Tau* and our own letter T is the very form of the cross, which He predicted would be the sign on our foreheads in the true Catholic Jerusalem, in which, according to the twenty-first Psalm, the brethren of Christ or children of God would ascribe glory to God the Father, in the person of Christ Himself addressing His Father: "I will declare Your name unto my brethren; in the midst of the congregation will I sing praise unto Thee."[7]

He also describes how frequently it was made by the early Christians: "At every forward step and movement, at every going in and out, when we put on our clothes and shoes, when we bathe, when we sit at table, when we light the lamps, on couch, on seat, in all the ordinary actions of daily life, we trace upon the forehead the sign." [8] Through the sign of the cross, prefigured in Old Testament prophecy and fulfilled in Christ, Christians proclaim their fidelity to the thrice-holy God, symbolized by the sign of the cross.

A century and a half later, St. Cyril of Jerusalem explained the sign of the cross to the newly-baptized Christians. It is, first of all, a confession of faith: "Let us not then be ashamed to confess the Crucified. Be the Cross our seal made with boldness by our fingers on our brow, and on everything."[9] It was still used by Christians to sanctify the moments and events of daily life: "over the bread we eat, and the cups we drink; in our comings in, and goings out; before our sleep, when we lie down and when we rise up; when we are in the way, and

---

7. Tertullian, *Against Marcion*, in vol. 3 of *The Ante-Nicene Fathers: Translations of The Writings of the Fathers Down to A.D. 325*, ed. Alexander Roberts, DD, and James Donaldson, LLD (Grand Rapids, MI: Eerdmans Publishing Company, 1980), 340–341.

8. Tertullian, *De Corona*, in vol. 3 of *The Ante-Nicene Fathers: Translations of The Writings of the Fathers Down to A.D. 325*, ed. Alexander Roberts, DD, and James Donaldson, LLD (Grand Rapids, MI: Eerdmans Publishing Company, 1980), 94–95.

9. Cyril of Jerusalem, "Catechetical Lectures, Lecture XIII," in *A Select Library of Nicene and Post-Nicene Fathers of the Christian Church*, Second Series, vol. 7, ed. Philip Schaff and Henry Wace (Grand Rapids, MI: Eerdman's Publishing Company, 1983), 92.

when we are still."[10] St. Cyril also described the power of the sign of the cross to keep Christians safe against the wiles and attacks of the enemy: "Great is that preservative; it is without price, for the sake of the poor; without toil, for the sick; since also its grace is from God. It is the Sign of the faithful, and the dread of devils: for He triumphed over them in it, having made a show of them openly [Col 2:15]; for when they see the Cross they are reminded of the Crucified; they are afraid of Him, who bruised the heads of the dragon. Despise not the Seal, because of the freeness of the gift; out for this the rather honor your Benefactor."[11] Through this simple gesture we too can profess our faith, sanctify the events of our daily life and invoke the power of God.

The sign of the cross, as with many liturgical signs, conveys a wealth of meaning. It is the mark of those zealous for the holiness and glory of God and a sign of the power of God displayed in the cross of Christ. St. Cyril's description of the sign of the cross as a great preservative and weapon against the enemy is a wonderful example of how a sacramental sign makes present the reality it signifies. The sign of the cross truly enables us to "enter into the power of the blessing of Christ."[12]

The Sign of the Cross in the Sacraments

Where, by whom, and how often is the sign of the cross made during the Mass?

What is the meaning of each of these Signs of the Cross?

Silence

Another, somewhat different kind of liturgical sign is silence. In its *Constitution on the Sacred Liturgy*, the Second Vatican Council listed it as one of the elements of active participation: "To promote active participation, the people should be encouraged to take part by means of acclamations, responses, psalmody, antiphons, and songs, as well as by actions, gestures, and bodily attitudes. And at the proper times all should observe a reverent silence" (SC, 30). Liturgical silence is not

---

10. Ibid.

11. Ibid.

12. Ratzinger, *Spirit*, 184.

merely an absence of words, nor is it simply a pause or interlude. "Rather, it is a stillness, a quieting of spirits, a taking time and leisure to hear, assimilate, and respond. . . . The dialogue between God and the community of faith taking place through the Holy Spirit requires intervals of silence, suited to the congregation, so that all can take to heart the word of God and respond to it in prayer" (IOM, 48). Note especially the language of relationship and encounter—hearing the word of God addressed to us, understanding it, and responding to the One who has addressed us. Silence, then, facilitates relationship with the Blessed Trinity and becomes a means to greater communion with the Father through the Son under the action of the Holy Spirit.

The purpose of liturgical silence varies. During the Mass, for example in the Penitential Rite and after the invitation to pray before the Collect, it provides an opportunity for personal recollection. Following the readings or the Homily it creates a space for meditation on the proclaimed word. Silence after Communion is a time for prayer and praise. "This, in all truth, is the moment for an interior conversation with the Lord who has given himself to us, for that essential 'communicating' . . . without which the external reception of the Sacrament becomes mere ritual and therefore unfruitful".[13] St. Teresa of Avila urged her nuns to spend time in prayer after receiving Communion: "Be with Him willingly; don't lose so good an occasion for conversing with Him as is the hour after having received Communion. . . . This, then, is a good time for our Master to teach us, and for us to listen to Him, kiss His feet because He wanted to teach us, and beg Him not to leave." "Why doubt," she asked, " if we have faith, that miracles will be worked while He is within us and that He will give what we ask of Him, since He is in our House? His Majesty is not accustomed to paying poorly for His lodging if the hospitality is good."[14] Silence at different moments in the liturgy develops our docility to the Holy Spirit.

Silence during the liturgy can be challenging, even uncomfortable. "Ours is not an age which fosters recollection; at times one has the impression that people are afraid of detaching themselves, even for a

---

13. Ibid., 210.

14. Teresa of Avila, *The Collected Works of Teresa of Avila*, trans. Kieran Kavanaugh, OCD, and Otilio Rodriguez, OCD, vol. 2, *The Way of Perfection, Meditations on the Song of Sons, The Interior Castle* (Washington, DC: ICS Publications, 1980), 172.

moment, from the mass media" (VD, 66). This calls for a special catechesis on the meaning of silence in the liturgy in order to rediscover "a
sense of recollection and inner repose. Only in silence can the word of
God find a home in us, as it did in Mary, woman of the word and,
inseparably, woman of silence. Our liturgies must facilitate this attitude
of authentic listening" (VD, 66). In the words of the great Spanish doctor St. John of the Cross, "The Father spoke one Word, which was his
Son, and this Word he speaks always in eternal silence, and in silence
must it be heard by the soul."[15]

Silence

The Church suggests silence during the Mass at seven
different points:

1. Prior to the beginning of Mass (GIRM, 45)

2. Prior to the Penitential Act (GIRM, 54)

3. After the invitation to pray (before the Collect) (GIRM, 54)

4. Before the Liturgy of the Word begins (GIRM, 56)

5. After the First and Second Readings (GIRM, 56)

6. After the homily (GIRM, 56)

7. After Communion

At which of these points is silence most meaningful for you?

Movement

Movement is another important liturgical sign. The prescribed movements of the ministers and people manifest important aspects of the
sacramental reality that is being celebrated. A good example is the
Sacrament of Baptism. One of the fruits of baptism is that the recipient
is incorporated into the Church of Christ. This sacramental reality is
manifested through the movements and stations of the rite, what one
might call the "geography" of the sacrament. It typically begins at the
entrance of the church signifying that one is asking for membership in

---

15. John of the Cross, *The Collected Works of St. John of the Cross*, trans. Kieran
Kavanaugh, OCD, and Otilio Rodriguez, OCD (Washington, DC: ICS Publications, 1991), 92.

the Church. Here all are welcomed, the parents are questioned, the child is signed on the forehead, the liturgy of the word is celebrated, followed by the prayer of exorcism and the prebaptismal anointing. At the entrance to the church these introductory rites prepare one for membership in the Church.

Following the anointing with the oil of catechumens, all go to the baptismal font for the celebration of the sacrament: the blessing of the baptism water, renunciation of sin and profession of faith, baptism, clothing with the white garment, presentation of the lighted candle, and the prayer over the ears and mouth. Through these rites the child's sins are forgiven, he or she is made a child of God, a temple of the Holy Spirit, and a member of Christ's Church. This sacramental reality is next signified by a procession to the altar, which also manifests the fact that baptism is oriented to Eucharistic communion. Here the assembly prays the Lord's Prayer, receives a blessing from the celebrant, and is dismissed. The Rite of Baptism thus takes place at three distinct stations—the entrance of the church, the baptismal font, and the altar—which physically manifest the spiritual reality being enacted.

Movement is also an important part of the Eucharist. The Mass includes four separate processions: the entrance procession, the procession with the Book of the Gospels, the procession with the gifts, and the communion procession. With the exception of the Gospel procession, all the processions begin in the nave and move to the sanctuary. This reflects the symbolism of the church building. The sanctuary is the fulfillment of the Old Testament holy of holies as well as an image of the heavenly Jerusalem, the dwelling place of God. The nave is the dwelling of the people of God. "In this perspective, procession represents the pilgrimage of the people of God to its heavenly homeland; it represents the union of God and man, begun now in grace, and progressing toward its perfection in glory."[16]

Let's look more closely at one of these processions, the procession with the gifts of bread, wine and money that follows the Prayers of the Faithful. It normally begins in the nave and moves to the sanctuary where the gifts are received by the priest. This procession manifests a rich symbolism. It expresses the congregation's participation in the Eucharist, an aspect that "is best expressed if the procession passes right

---

16. John Mary Burns, "The Procession of the *Ordo Missae*: Liturgical Structure and Theological Meaning", *Antiphon* 13, no. 2 (2009): 162.

through their midst" (IOM, 105). It also manifests "the humble and contrite heart, the dispossession of self that is necessary for making the true offering, which the Lord Jesus gave his people to make for him. The procession with the gifts expresses also our eager willingness to enter into the 'holy exchange' with God: 'accept the offerings you have given us, that we in turn may receive the gift of yourself [Prayer over Offerings]'" (IOM, 105).

This procession is also a form of intercession for the world, as Pope Benedict XVI explains:

> This humble and simple gesture is actually very significant: in the bread and wine that we bring to the altar, all creation is taken up by Christ the Redeemer to be transformed and presented to the Father. In this way we also bring to the altar all the pain and suffering of the world, in the certainty that everything has value in God's eyes" (SacCar, 47).

So what can appear as a strictly functional action is in fact a movement of profound spiritual meaning and power. It expresses the participation of the assembly in the Mass, the humility and contrition of the people of God, their willingness to offer themselves, and their intercession for the whole world.

Movement then is one of the ways that the liturgy engages the whole person. It also reveals the sacramentality of the church building and effects its participation in the liturgy. It reminds us that here we are "aliens and sojourners" (1 Pt 2:11) whose "citizenship is in heaven" (Phil 3:20) toward which we journey as God's "pilgrim Church on earth" (Eucharistic Prayer III). Finally, liturgical movement helps form in us the proper dispositions for fruitful participation in sacramental celebrations.

Incense

The liturgy also makes use of different kinds of material signs, for example, water, oil, and bread. Incense is one of the material signs used in a number of liturgical celebrations. It is recommended for more solemn celebrations of the Eucharist, during exposition and benediction of the Blessed Sacrament, in the rite of dedication of a church and altar, at solemn celebrations of Morning Prayer and Evening Prayer, funerals, and "in any procession of some solemnity" (CB, 88). Incense is another kind of liturgical language, another way that the liturgy engages the whole person, for it appeals to our senses of sight and smell. For this reason, the Church encourages its use "in amounts sufficient to be seen and smelled" (IOM, 58).

As a liturgical sign, incense is rich in meanings. First and foremost, it is a sign of prayer. This meaning is rooted in the Old and New Testaments. The psalmist begged God, "Let my prayer be counted as incense before you" (Ps 141:2). St. John saw it used in the heavenly liturgy: "Another angel came and stood at the altar with a golden censer; and he was given much incense to mingle with the prayers of all the saints upon the golden altar before the throne" (Rev 8:3). It also symbolizes the Church's gifts rising to the Father. During the Mass, the gifts on the altar as well as the cross and altar are incensed "so as to signify the Church's offering and prayer rising like incense in the sight of God" (GIRM, 75). Then, as a sign of dignity, "the Priest, because of his sacred ministry, and the people, by reason of their baptismal dignity, may be incensed by the Deacon or by another minister" (GIRM, 75). Incense is also an expression of reverence, "a sign of respect and honor" before Christ (IOM, 58). In addition, it recalls the pillar of cloud (Ex 13:21) by which God led Israel in the wilderness, the cloud itself symbolizing "God's glory and presence in the midst of the Israelites" (IOM, 58). In this way it "suggests both the otherness of the transcendent God and . . . can contribute powerfully to a sense of mystery" (IOM, 58).

The use of incense in the liturgy expresses many meanings. It signifies the prayers and gifts of the assembly rising up to God. It acknowledges Christ present as Head (in the ordained minister) and Body (all the baptized). It is a sign of the dignity of the ordained ministers and the priesthood of the baptized who together celebrate the liturgy as Christ Head and Body. It engages yet another of our senses, contributing to the participation of the whole person. Finally, it conveys reverence for Christ and the transcendent otherness of God present in the midst of his people, enriching the solemnity and mystery of the liturgy.

> ## Incense
>
> During the Mass, for example, incense can be used at five points: the entrance procession, the introductory rites, the proclamation of the Gospel, the preparation of the gifts, and the elevation of the sacred species following the consecration.
>
> What is the significance of incense at each of these points?

Liturgical Colors

The last liturgical sign we will examine is color. Pope Innocent III (1160/61–1216) first determined specific colors for specific days, and his choices are essentially those still in force today: white, red, green and black. However, it wasn't until the Missal of 1570 that an obligatory liturgical color scheme first appeared. The approved liturgical colors in the United States are white, red, green, violet or purple, black and rose (GIRM, 346). Gold and silver are approved for use in the United States "on more solemn occasions" (GIRM, 346). In the liturgy, colors contribute to the expression of "the specific character of the mysteries of faith to be celebrated" (GIRM, 345), which we will now consider.

White is a symbol of God, who dwells in unapproachable light (1 Tim 6:16) and of Christ, "the light of the world" (JN 8:12). Therefore, it is used during Christmas Time, Easter Time, the Solemnity of the Most Holy Trinity, celebrations of the Lord (except for the Passion). It is also a sign of purity, so it is also used for celebrations of the Blessed Virgin Mary, of the Holy Angels, and of the Saints who were not martyrs. It is also used on a few other liturgical celebrations such as the Solemnity of All Saints (November 1) and the feast of the Conversion of St. Paul (January 25).[17] Finally, white is a sign of joy, and so it is used in processions with the Blessed Sacrament, and in the Sacraments of Baptism, Confirmation (or red), Anointing of the Sick and Viaticum.

---

17. Liturgical celebrations are categorized according to their importance. First in importance are solemnities, such as the Immaculate Conception of the Blessed Virgin Mary (December 8), which begin on the evening of the preceding day. Next in importance are feasts, such as the Feast of the Transfiguration (August 6). Third in rank are memorials, which are either obligatory or optional.

The joy of the angels at the birth of Christ, his resurrection victory over sin and death, the radiance of the Blessed Trinity and the purity and radiance of the saints all find liturgical expression in the color white.

Like the color white, the color red also signifies diverse aspects of the faith. It is the color of fire, which is one of the biblical images of the Holy Spirit (Acts 2:3), so it is used on Pentecost Sunday and in the celebration of the Sacrament of Confirmation within the Mass. As the color of blood, it signifies the suffering of the Lord and the saints, so it is also used on Palm Sunday, Good Friday, celebrations of the Lord's Passion, on the "birthday" feast days of the Apostles and Evangelists, and on the celebrations of saints who were martyred. The color red is a sign to us of Christ's suffering with us and for us, of the faithful and courageous testimony of the martyrs, and of "the Gift that contains all gifts, the Holy Spirit" (CCC, 1082).

Green, the color of springtime, new growth, and hope, is used in Ordinary Time, especially "in the ordinary Sundays of the year, which are commemorations of the great Sunday of the Resurrection, when hope once again returned to the world."[18] The color violet or purple is a sign of sorrow, mourning, penance, and repentance. Thus, it is used in Advent and Lent, as well as in the Sacrament of Penance. Rose, a sign of subdued joy, is used during the penitential seasons of Advent (*Gaudete* Sunday, the Third Sunday of Advent) and Lent (*Laetare* Sunday, the Fourth Sunday of Lent). Although white is most commonly worn at funerals, violet and black, a symbol of mourning and death, are also permitted.

In addition to expressing the specific character of the liturgical mysteries, liturgical colors also give "a sense of Christian life's passage through the course of the liturgical year" (GIRM, 345). "In the liturgical year the various aspects of the one Paschal mystery unfold" (CCC, 1171). In the course of the liturgical year the Church recalls "the mysteries of redemption . . . [and] opens to the faithful the riches of her Lord's powers and merits, so that these are in some way made present for all time, and the faithful are enabled to lay hold upon them and become filled with saving grace" (SC, 102). However, the liturgical year, which begins with Advent, does not unfold in a strictly chronological order

---

18. Virgil Michel, OSB, *The Liturgy of the Church* (New York: MacMillan, 1937), 77.

(if it did, Easter would be celebrated at the end of the year rather than in the middle). Rather, taking

> the Easter Triduum as its source of light, the new age of the Resurrection fills the whole liturgical year with its brilliance. Gradually, on either side of this source, the year is transfigured by the liturgy. It really is a 'year of the Lord's favor.' The economy of salvation is at work within the framework of time, but since its fulfillment in the Passover of Jesus and the outpouring of the Holy Spirit, the culmination of history is anticipated 'as a foretaste,' and the kingdom of God enters into our time" (CCC, 1168).

This unfolding of time now transfigured by the "new age of the Resurrection" finds expression in the liturgical use of color. The brilliance of the Resurrection is signified by the use of white, gold or silver throughout the season of Easter. The use of violet or purple in the forty days leading up to the Triduum assist us in preparing for the great event through sorrow, contrition and penance. The green of Ordinary Time that precedes Lent and follows Easter is a sign of hope and faith as the events of our Lord's life that find their definitive power and fulfillment in the age of the Resurrection and the riches of our Lord's powers and merits are made liturgically present. Finally, the overflowing radiance of the Triduum reaches back to the penitential and expectant character of Advent, expressed through the use of violet/purple vestments, while also reaching forward to the radiant culmination of the liturgical year, the Solemnity of Christ the King, symbolized by white, silver, or gold. In this way we see how the liturgical colors visually express our pilgrim journey toward our heavenly homeland.

Liturgical colors combine with the other liturgical signs to make present the various aspects of the one Paschal Mystery. They characterize the central mystery of our faith, the Paschal Mystery. Within the major seasons of the liturgical year—Advent, Christmas, Ordinary Time, Lent, Easter—are expressed the individual events and mysteries of the life of Christ and the saints. In the liturgy, colors contribute to the expression of "the specific character of the mysteries of faith to be celebrated" (GIRM, 345), aiding us in entering into the liturgy with our whole being.

Liturgical Color

What is the liturgical color for each of the following celebrations?

The Assumption (August 15)

Triumph of the Cross (September 14)

The Lord's Supper (Holy Thursday)

Christ the King (Last Sunday in Ordinary Time)

The Sacred Heart (Friday following the Second Sunday after Pentecost)

THE ESSENTIAL RITE

For centuries the Church, using the language of medieval Scholastic theology, identified two elements as necessary for the celebration of each sacrament, the *matter* and the *form*. The matter is the required visible, material element (e.g., water for Baptism, grape wine and unleavened wheat bread for the Eucharist), and the form is the prayer that accompanies and explains the matter. However, these two elements are not equally clear in every sacrament. For example, in the case of the Sacrament of Penance and Reconciliation the matter "is not so straightforward because there is no immediately visible element upon which the creative word [the form] can confer a salvific meaning."[19] The Church considers the acts of the penitent—confession, contrition and satisfaction—the quasi-matter (quasi meaning "as it were"[20]) of the sacrament. Similarly, the Sacrament of Marriage lacks a visible element that constitutes the matter: "the matter is the mutual self-giving of the spouses, and the form is the mutual acceptance of this self-giving."[21] As these examples illustrate, the terms *matter* and *form* more clearly describe the key elements of some sacraments than of others.

The *Catechism of the Catholic Church* does not use the language of matter and form, referring instead to the "essential rite." For example,

---

19. Paul Haffner, *The Sacramental Mystery*, rev. ed. (Herefordshire, UK: Gracewing, 2007), 152.

20. Ibid., 153.

21. Ibid., 243–244.

the essential rite for Baptism is the triple immersion in the baptismal water, or the triple pouring of water—the matter, along with the words, "N. I baptize you in the name of the Father, and of the Son, and of the Holy Spirit"—the form (CCC, 1239–1240). If the "essential rite" is changed or omitted, the sacrament is invalid; in other words, it did not take place. When discussing the individual sacraments, we will use the language of the *Catechism*, the essential rite, rather than the scholastic language of matter and form.

HARMONY OF SIGNS

While the individual liturgical signs constitute a complex liturgical language that appeals to different senses and engages the whole person, they also combine in a harmonious way to make present in all of its richness the one Paschal Mystery of Christ. For this reason, the *Catechism* speaks of "the harmony of signs" (1158), the way that words and silence, movement and gesture, song and music, sight and smell, combine to make present in its fullness the Paschal Mystery.

The *Catechism* cites the contemplation of sacred icons as an example of this harmony of signs: "the contemplation of sacred icons, united with meditation on the Word of God and the singing of liturgical hymns, enters into the harmony of the signs of the celebration so that the mystery celebrated is imprinted in the heart's memory and is then expressed in the new life of the faithful" (CCC, 1162). Here we see how three liturgical signs—sacred images, Sacred Scripture, and liturgical song—together make present a specific event ("the mystery celebrated") from the life of our Lord (e.g., the Nativity, the Transfiguration, or the Resurrection) or the Blessed Virgin Mary (e.g., the Annunciation, the Visitation, or the Crucifixion) that can transform the life of the faithful.

While we have considered examples of the different kinds of signs that comprise the language of the liturgy, these elements do not occur in isolation. Rather, they combine in distinct but complementary ways to make present the one Paschal Mystery of Christ through which the Father draws us into the Trinitarian life of love through his beloved Son in the Holy Spirit. The more we can understand and appreciate the meaning and harmony of the different signs, the more effectively are we able to participate full, actively and consciously in the liturgy for our sanctification and the glory of God.

Harmony of Signs

An example of this harmony of signs that is familiar to all Catholics is the Communion Rite of the Mass. Receiving the Body and Blood of the Lord "in a paschal meal is the culmination of the Eucharist" (IOM, 125). the Communion Rite is composed of the following elements: The Lord's Prayer, the Rite of Peace, the Fraction Rite, Communion (including procession), the Communion Chant, and the Prayer after Communion. While each element is rich in meaning, "in the context of the whole celebration they constitute together a transition from one high point, the Eucharistic Prayer, to another, the sharing in Holy Communion" (IOM, 125).

1. Which of the liturgical signs and symbols discussed in chapters 1 and 2 are present in the Communion Rite? Consider such things as words, silence, movement, color, posture, images, song.

2. How do these different liturgical signs contribute to the effectiveness of this part of the Mass?

3. What might hinder or disrupt the harmony of signs?

CONCLUSION

In one of his letters on Holy Thursday St. John Paul II encouraged pastors to instruct the faithful on the meaning of the signs and symbols of the liturgy "by which the faithful are helped to understand the meaning of the liturgy's words and actions, to pass from its signs to the mystery which they contain, and to enter into that mystery in every aspect of their lives" (MND, 17). This exhortation eloquently summarizes the dynamic nature of the language of the liturgy. The signs and symbols of the liturgy "contain" the mystery that they signify. However, it is only when we understand the liturgical signs and symbols that we are able "to pass from its signs to the mystery they contain," for "when minds are enlightened and hearts are enkindled, signs begin to 'speak'" (MND, 14). This is the essence of full, active and conscious participation in the liturgy, passing from its visible signs to an encounter with the Blessed Trinity and the power of the Paschal Mystery which they contain and make present.

Chapter 3

From Sign to Mystery: Mystagogical Catechesis

As we have seen in the preceding chapters, through the faith of the Church and the power of the Holy Spirit, God communicates the fruits of Christ's Paschal Mystery to us by means of a rich and varied liturgical language that engages the whole person. The challenge for us today is mastering the language of the liturgy, a task that "is particularly important in a highly technological age like our own, which risks losing the ability to appreciate signs and symbols" (SacCar, 64). It is the task of liturgical catechists to "initiate people into the mystery of Christ by proceeding from the visible to the invisible, from the sign to the thing signified, from the 'sacraments' to the 'mysteries'" (CCC, 1075). This type of catechesis is called *mystagogy*, from the Greek word for the person who led an initiate into a mystery. Its goal is to lead people from the signs to the spiritual realities they signify.

Recent popes have encouraged this kind of catechesis. In *Stay With Us Lord*, St. John Paul II wrote, "Pastors should be committed to that *'mystagogical' catechesis* so dear to the Fathers of the Church, by which the faithful are helped to understand the meaning of the liturgy's words and actions, to pass from its signs to the mystery which they contain, and to enter into that mystery in every aspect of their lives" (MND, 17). He affirms the theme of the previous chapter: liturgical signs contain the mystery they signify. Pope Francis, speaking specifically of the sacraments of initiation, has also encouraged a mystagogical approach to catechesis that involves the whole community and opens up the meaning of liturgical signs. Such an approach, writes Pope Francis, should be part of "a broader growth process and the integration of every dimension of the person within a communal journey of hearing and response" (EG, 166). Understanding the words and actions of the liturgy enables us to pass from the outward signs and actions of the liturgy to the spiritual reality and power they contain. The sacraments have the power to utterly transform every aspect of our lives.

Mystagogical catechesis is a part of the Church's Tradition, a method of catechesis "so dear to the Fathers of the Church" (MND, 17). In the first centuries of the Church, following the reception of the sacraments of initiation—Baptism, a post-baptismal anointing which we know as Confirmation, and first Eucharist—the new Christians were given a detailed catechesis explaining the meaning of the sacraments and the significance of the words and actions of the rite they had just received. The purpose of mystagogical catechesis was not to prepare people to receive the sacraments, but rather to help them understand more deeply the sacraments they had just received. The fourth century was the golden age of mystagogical catechesis. From this period we have important mystagogical texts from such illustrious Church Fathers as St. Cyril of Jerusalem (d. 386), St. Ambrose (d. 397), and St. John Chrysostom (d. 407). The writings of the Church Fathers continue to instruct us about the meaning of the sacraments and constitute an important source for our exploration of the sacraments.

Pope Benedict XVI expanded St. John Paul II's emphasis on catechesis that leads people into the mystery. In *Sacrament of Charity* (64), he proposed a model of mystagogical catechesis consisting of three elements.

1. *"It interprets the rites in the light of the events of our salvation*, in accordance with the Church's living tradition. . . . From the beginning, the Christian community has interpreted the events of Jesus' life, and the Paschal Mystery in particular, in relation to the entire history of the Old Testament."

2. Mystagogical catechesis explains *"the meaning of the signs* contained in the rites."

3. It should emphasize "the *significance of the rites for the Christian life* in all its dimensions—work and responsibility, thoughts and emotions, activity and repose." Ultimately, this kind of catechesis should lead to "an awareness that one's life is being progressively transformed by the holy mysteries being celebrated."

OLD TESTAMENT ROOTS

The first part of a mystagogical catechesis is to explain the rite in the light of its Old Testament roots. The sacraments of the Church are prefigured by the Old Testament persons (Adam, Joseph, Isaac, and David, for example, prefigured in different ways the person and work of Christ) and events, such as anointing, the consecration of kings and priests, sacrifices, the laying on of hands, and above all the Passover. "The Church sees in these signs a prefiguring of the sacraments of the New Covenant" (CCC, 1150). The persons and events of the Old Testament point to the mysteries of Christ and reveal different aspects of his Paschal Mystery, "for he himself is the meaning of all of these signs" (CCC, 1151). There are three readily available sources that reveal the Old Testament roots of each sacrament:

- the rite itself
- the biblical readings proscribed in the rite for each sacrament
- the *Catechism of the Catholic Church*

The Rite Itself

The rite itself is always the best starting point, for these are the words we hear and say, the gestures and postures we adopt, and the signs and symbols that engage us, and that lead us deeper into the mystery of the sacrament. The liturgy is one of the primary ways that the Church has passed on the faith entrusted to her by the Lord. Christ has entrusted to the Church the responsibility of passing "on the faith in its integrity so that the 'rule of prayer' (*lex orandi*) of the church may correspond to the 'rule of faith' (*lex credendi*)" (VL, 27). The terms "rule of prayer" (*lex orandi*) and "rule of faith" (*lex credendi*) refer to a principle that dates back to Prosper of Aquitaine (fifth century). The *Catechism of the Catholic Church* explains this principle: "The law of prayer is the law of faith: the Church believes as she prays. Liturgy is a constitutive element of the holy and living Tradition" (1124). Another Church Father, St. Irenaeus (late second century), expressed this principle with respect to the Mass: "Our way of thinking is attuned to the Eucharist, and the Eucharist in turn confirms our way of thinking" (CCC, 1327). From the earliest days the Church has understood the inseparable relationship between her worship and her faith, and for this reason the sacramental rite is always the best starting point for understanding the meaning of the sacrament itself.

An excellent example of this is Eucharistic Prayer I (the Roman Canon) from the Mass. Following the consecration, there is a prayer asking God to accept "these offerings . . . as once you were pleased to accept the gifts of your servant Abel the just, the sacrifice of Abraham, our father in faith, and the offering of your high priest Melchizedek." Let us look closely at the last example, "the offering of your high priest Melchizedek." This event is recounted in Genesis 14:17–20. Melchizedek, the king of Salem, meets Abraham as he is returning victorious from battle. Melchizedek is described as a priest, and he brings bread and wine and blesses Abraham, who then gives Melchizedek a tenth of the spoils. St. Cyprian (d. 258) described Melchizedek as "a type of Christ" (an identification that is extensively developed in the Letter to the Hebrews). Cyprian emphasizes Melchizedek's offering of bread and wine and his blessing of Abraham. "For who is more a priest of the most high God," he asks, "than our Lord Jesus Christ, who offered sacrifice to God the Father and offered the very same thing that Melchizedek had offered, bread and wine, that is, actually, his body and blood?"[1]

Prefigurement of the Eucharist in the Old Testament

Read the accounts of "the gifts of Abel" (Gen 4:1–16) and "the sacrifice of Abraham" (Gen 22:1–19). In what ways do these reveal different aspects of the Eucharist?

The Biblical Readings for Each Sacrament

Each sacrament includes suggested Old Testament readings, responsorial psalms, passages from the New Testament epistles, and appropriate selections from the Gospels, all chosen to highlight different aspects of the sacrament being celebrated. For example, one of the Old Testament options for the ordination of bishops and priests is Isaiah 61:1–3a. In this passage the prophet announces that he is the anointed messenger empowered by the spirit of the Lord to announce freedom, healing, and salvation to God's afflicted. In the Gospel of Luke, Jesus inaugurates his public ministry by reading this passage in the synagogue. It is a fitting passage for the ordination of bishops and priests, who through the gift

---

1. Mark Sheridan, ed., *Genesis 12–50*, Ancient Christian Commentary on Scripture (Downers Grove, IL: InterVaristy Press, 2002), 26.

of the Spirit are configured "to Christ as Priest, Teacher, and Pastor, of whom the ordained is made a minister" (CCC, 1585).

Catechism of the Catholic Church

A third source for exploring the Old Testament roots of each sacrament is the *Catechism of the Catholic Church*. As an example, let's look at the Sacrament of Confirmation. The *Catechism* finds the Old Testament roots of this sacrament in the prophetic announcement of the Spirit-anointed Messiah in Isaiah 11:2: "And the spirit of the LORD shall rest upon him: a spirit of wisdom and of understanding, a spirit of counsel and of strength, a spirit of knowledge and of fear of the LORD" (CCC, 1286).[2] The descent of the Spirit upon Jesus at his baptism is the sign that he is the fulfillment of Isaiah's prophecy. The prophecies of two other Old Testament figures, Ezekiel (36:25–27) and Joel (3:1–2), affirm that the Spirit was to be given "to the *whole messianic people*" (CCC, 1287). "From that time on the apostles, in fulfillment of Christ's will, imparted to the newly baptized by the laying on of hands the gift of the Spirit that completes the grace of Baptism" (CCC, 1288).

Let's take a more detailed look at an example of the Old Testament roots of Baptism as found in the rite itself in the blessing of the baptismal waters. The prayer begins as follows (I have included the rubric, which is an important sacramental sign [described in chapter 1]).

> *With hands outstretched he says:*
>
> O God, who by invisible power
> accomplish a wondrous effect
> through sacramental signs
> and who in many ways have prepared water, your creation,
> to show forth the grace of Baptism . . .
> (RM, Easter Vigil, Blessing of Baptismal Water, 46).

This opening stanza concisely expresses the sacramental principle: God communicates the power and fruits of the Paschal Mystery to us through sacramental signs to "accomplish a wondrous effect." As we discussed in chapter 2, God mediates his presence to us through signs and symbols taken from human culture, the Old Testament, and, in the case of Baptism, creation itself—water. This stanza further explains

---

2. The earliest reference we have to this passage as included in the prayer that accompanies the imposition of hands is St. Ambrose (d. 397).

that God has used water "in many ways" to express the grace of Baptism. The succeeding stanzas will give three different Old Testament examples of how God prepared water "to show forth the grace of Baptism." Each stanza cites one Old Testament example and explains how it reveals a specific aspect of Baptism.

The first Old Testament event cited in this prayer is the account of creation in Genesis 1.

> O God, whose Spirit
> in the first moments of the world's creation
> hovered over the waters,
> so that the very substance of water
> would even then take to itself the power to sanctify . . .
> (RM, Easter Vigil, Blessing of Baptismal Water, 46).

The reference here is to Genesis 1:2: "the Spirit of God was moving over the face of the waters" (RSVCE translation). The Spirit moving over the waters is seen as a sort of primordial epiclesis (see chapter 1) in which the Spirit imparts to water the power to sanctify. St. Jerome (d. 420) saw in this passage a prefiguration of Baptism: "already at that time baptism was being foreshadowed."[3] Tertullian (d. ca. 220), in his interpretation of this passage from Genesis, specifically emphasized the power of water to sanctify: "The Holy One was carried over that which was holy, or, rather, over that which could receive holiness from Him Who was carried. It is thus that the nature of water, sanctified by the Spirit, received the capability of itself becoming sanctifying. This is why all waters, by reason of their ancient original prerogative, may obtain the sacrament of sanctification [Baptism] by the invocation of God."[4] Through the power of the Spirit, material substances such as water can receive the power to convey holiness.

The prayer next invokes the flood as described in Genesis 6 and 7.

> O God, who by the outpouring of the flood
> foreshadowed regeneration,
> so that from the mystery of one and the same element of water
> would come an end to vice and a beginning of virtue . . .
> (RM, Easter Vigil, Blessing of Baptismal Water, 46).

---

3. Andrew Louth, ed., *Genesis 1–11*, Ancient Christian Commentary on Scripture (Downers Grove, IL: InterVarsity Academic Press, 2001), 6.

4. Jean Daniélou, SJ, *The Bible and the Liturgy* (Notre Dame, IN: University of Notre Dame Press, 1956), 72–73.

God, grieved by the wickedness of mankind, sent a flood to blot out all vice while preserving life through Noah, who was righteous and blameless (Gen 6:9). St. Augustine saw in the flood a prefigurement of Baptism: "Who does not know, indeed, that in other times the earth was purified from its stains by the Flood. And that the mystery of holy Baptism, by which all the sins of man were cleansed by the water, was preached already beforehand?"[5] Through Baptism our sins are forgiven and the gift of the Spirit enables us to live a life of holiness for God.

The final Old Testament reference in the prayer of blessing is Israel's exodus from Egypt recounted in Exodus 14.

> O God, who caused the children of Abraham
> to pass dry-shod through the Red Sea,
> so that the chosen people,
> set free from slavery to Pharaoh,
> would prefigure the people of the baptized . . .
> (RM, Easter Vigil, Blessing of Baptismal Water, 46).

St. Paul, in his First Letter to the Corinthians, interpreted the exodus from Egypt as a type of Baptism: "all passed through the sea, and all of them were baptized into Moses in the cloud and in the sea" (10:1–2). St. Basil the Great developed this interpretation: "The sea is the figure of Baptism, since it delivered the people from Pharaoh, as Baptism from the tyranny of the devil. The sea killed the enemy; so in Baptism, our enmity to God is destroyed. The people came out of the sea whole and safe; we also come out of the water as living men from among the dead."[6] St. Gregory of Nyssa also saw in the Exodus a figure of Baptism: "when the people approach the water of rebirth as they flee from Egypt, which is sin, they themselves are freed and saved, but the devil and his aids, the spirits of wickedness, are destroyed."[7] Baptism, then, frees us from slavery to sin just as the Exodus freed the chosen people from slavery to Pharaoh.

These three Old Testament passages reveal important aspects of the Sacrament of Baptism. From creation we learn that the baptismal waters receive from the Spirit the power to sanctify believers. Baptism, like the Flood, brings an end to the reign of sin and the

---

5. Ibid., 279.
6. Ibid., 90.
7. Ibid.

beginning of holiness. Finally, Baptism, like the Exodus, frees us from slavery to sin and brings us into "the glorious freedom of the children of God" (Rom 8:21).

MYSTAGOGICAL CATECHESIS: MEANING OF THE SIGNS

An effective mystagogical catechesis *explains the meaning of the different signs contained in the rites.* The liturgical signs are essential because they are "bearers of the saving and sanctifying action of Christ" (CCC, 1189). Furthermore, we need to understand these signs, because only when we understand them are we able to pass from the signs to the mystery they contain. The sacraments differ in their complexity and in the number and variety of the signs and symbols. The Mass, for example, employs a greater number of liturgical signs than the Sacrament of Penance and Reconciliation. In addition, while many signs are common to many if not all of the sacraments (see again chapter 2), each sacrament has some elements that are unique to that sacrament.

To illustrate this, let's look at three sacramental signs that comprise the ordination of a priest: vesting with stole and chasuble, anointing with sacred chrism, and the presentation of the paten and chalice. These three elements follow the imposition of hands and the Prayer of Consecration, the essential elements that "make" the sacrament, and so they are called "explanatory rites" since they explain the meaning of the sacrament just received. We'll begin with the vesting with stole and chasuble.

Immediately after the Prayer of Consecration, the newly ordained priest is vested with stole and chasuble, assisted by some of the priests present. The stole was originally a sort of protective towel or scarf which became a symbol of priestly authority, worn around the neck and falling in vertical strips in front. Current liturgical law stipulates that the stole be worn underneath the chasuble. The chasuble began as the outdoor cloak worn by citizens of the Greco-Roman world until the fifth century. It was originally a large square or circular garment with a hole cut in the middle for the wearer's head, hence the name chasuble, from the Latin word *casula*, meaning "little house." St. Isidore of Seville in the seventh century described it as "a garment furnished with a hood, which is a diminutive of *casa*, a cottage, as, like a small cottage or hut, it covers the entire person."[8] By the tenth century the chasuble was seen as a symbol of charity, as St. Ivo of Chartres (d. 1116) explained: "Over all the vestments is superimposed the chasuble . . . which, because it is the common vestment, signifies charity, which is superimposed over all the virtues [see Col 3:12–14], for the other virtues produce nothing profitable without it."[9] The chasuble is worn over the stole because "in the context of celebrating the Eucharistic Sacrifice, this symbol of charity should surely take precedence over the symbol of authority."[10] For priests the stole and chasuble outwardly manifest "the ministry they will henceforth fulfill in the Liturgy" (RO, 113).

The newly ordained are next anointed with chrism, which is made from olive oil or another plant oil mixed with an aromatic substance such as balsam and is consecrated only by a bishop. In addition to the Sacrament of Holy Orders, it is used in the Sacraments of Baptism and Confirmation. It "is a sign that Christians, incorporated by Baptism into the Paschal Mystery of Christ, dying, buried, and rising with him, are sharers in his kingly and prophetic Priesthood and that by Confirmation they receive the spiritual anointing of the Spirit who is given to them."[11] The *Rite for the Consecration of Chrism* summarizes the meaning of chrism. The bishop begins by inviting the people to ask God to "bless this oil so that all who are anointed with it may be inwardly transformed and come to share in eternal salvation."[12] Chrism, in all of its sacramental uses, is a sign and means of inner transformation through the Holy Spirit and so contributes to our salvation.

The bishop has a choice of two prayers for consecrating chrism. Each reveals different aspects of the meaning and power of the chrism. The first prayer asks the Father to "fill it with the power of your Holy Spirit through Christ your Son."[13] This prayer also explains that the name chrism is derived from Christ: "It is from him that Chrism takes its name and with Chrism you have anointed for yourself Priests and

---

8. Herbert Thurston, "Chasuble," in *The Catholic Encyclopedia* (New York: Robert Appleton, 1908), 639.

9. James Monti, *A Sense of the Sacred: Roman Catholic Worship in the Middle Ages* (San Francisco: Ignatius, 2012), 169.

10. Peter J. Elliott, *Ceremonies of the Modern Roman Rite: The Eucharist and the Liturgy of the Hours*, rev. ed. (San Francisco: Ignatius, 1995), 46.

11. "Introduction," *The Rite for the Blessing of Oils and the Consecration of Chrism*, 2.

12. Ibid.

13. Ibid.

kings, Prophets and Martyrs."[14] This prayer emphasizes its use in the Sacrament of Baptism: "Make this Chrism sign of life and salvation for those who are to be born again in the waters of Baptism."[15]

The second prayer explains how in the Old Testament God "gave your people a glimpse of the power of this holy oil" and then "brought that mystery to perfection in the life of our Lord Jesus Christ."[16] Henceforth, "through the sign of holy Chrism, you dispense your life and love to men." The prayer then asks, "Father, by the power of your love, make this mixture of oil and perfume a sign and source + of your blessing. . . . Above all, Father, we pray that through this sign of your anointing you will grant increase to your Church until it reaches the eternal glory."[17] Each of the sacraments that includes anointing with chrism gives increase to the Church: Baptism, which incorporates new members into the Body of Christ; Confirmation, which equips believers with the gifts of the Spirit to participate fully in the mission of the Church; and Holy Orders, through which the faithful are instructed in the authentic faith of the Apostles and sanctified chiefly through the Eucharist and Penance. This prayer offers a beautiful summary of the power of this liturgical sign: "Let the splendor of holiness shine on the world from every place and thing signed with this oil."[18]

The newly ordained priests are anointed while kneeling before the consecrating bishop. Kneeling as a liturgical sign has many meanings. In Old Testament thought, the knees were a symbol of strength: "to bend the knee is, therefore, to bend our strength before the living God, an acknowledgement of the fact that all that we are we receive from him."[19] In several Old Testament passages—2 Chron 6:13; Ezr 9:5; Ps 22:29—it is also an expression of worship. In the Middle Ages it was also a sign of homage.[20] "One kneels as a human gesture of submission. In Christian tradition, kneeling is an acknowledgment of one's creatureliness before God. It can signify penitence for sin, humility, reverence, and adora-

---

14. Ibid.

15. Ibid.

16. Ibid.

17. Ibid.

18. Ibid.

19. Ratzinger, *Spirit*, 191.

20. United States Conference of Catholic Bishops, *Praying with Body, Mind, and Voice* (Washington, DC: United States Conference of Catholic Bishops, 2010).

tion" (IOM, 31). In the ordination rite, it signifies the obedience of priests to the bishop. Newly ordained priests are anointed on the palms their hands. While performing the anointing, the bishop says the following words: "The Lord Jesus Christ, whom the Father anointed with the Holy Spirit and power, guard and preserve you that you may sanctify the Christian people and offer sacrifice to God" (RO, 133). This anointing "symbolizes the Priests' distinctive participation in Christ's Priesthood" (RO, 113).

Following the anointing, the bishop presents to the new priests a paten holding the bread and a chalice containing wine mixed with water for the celebration of the Mass. As the bishop hands them to the newly ordained, he says, "Receive the oblation of the holy people, to be offered to God. Understand what you do, imitate what you celebrate, and conform your life to the mystery of the Lord's Cross" (RO, 163). The priest will spend the rest of his earthly life fulfilling this command—understanding the profound spiritual reality of the Holy Sacrifice of the Mass, imitating Christ's gift of himself made present at every Mass, and conforming his life ever more completely to Christ's Paschal Mystery. This rite signifies priests' "duty of presiding at the celebration of the Eucharist and of following Christ crucified" (RO, 113).

These three sacramental signs—vesting with stole and chasuble, anointing with chrism and the presentation of the paten and chalice—signify essential aspects of the priesthood: authority exercised in charity, participation in the one priesthood of Christ, and the celebration of the Eucharist.

SIGNIFICANCE OF THE RITES FOR CHRISTIAN LIFE

The third aspect of effective mystagogical catechesis brings "out the *significance of the rites for the Christian life* in all its dimensions—work and responsibility, thoughts and emotions, activity and repose. Part of the mystagogical process is to demonstrate how the mysteries celebrated in the rite are linked to the missionary responsibility of the faithful. The mature fruit of mystagogy is an awareness that one's life is being progressively transformed by the holy mysteries being celebrated" (SacCar, 64). The sacraments both invite and enable us to conform our lives to the image of Christ.

SACRAMENTAL GRACE

The sacraments have the power to transform our lives because they communicate God's grace to us. The *Catechism* defines grace as "the *free and undeserved help* that God gives us to respond to his call to become children of God, adoptive sons, partakers of the divine nature and of eternal life" (CCC, 1996). It is "a *participation in the life of God*" that "introduces us into the intimacy of Trinitarian life" (CCC, 1997). Grace is "the gift of the Spirit who justifies and sanctifies us," but it also includes gifts that are proper to each of the sacraments, which is our concern here (CCC, 2003). The gifts or graces that are specific to each sacrament are signified by the corresponding sacramental signs, because each liturgical sign "points to what it specifically signifies."[21] For example, the Eucharistic bread and wine are signs of the Body and Blood of Christ. Furthermore, "the sacraments are given to us humans for the 'different situations of our life,' and consequently they must contain different effects of grace."[22] Put another way, "the grace imparted by the sacraments renders God's love, presence and power available in the present moment, in a way that is specific to each sacrament."[23] Marriage is the commitment today and always of man and wife to each other and to Christ"[24] Through the gifts specific to each sacrament, God bestows on us the love and power to deepen our participation in the life of the Trinity.

However, it is also true that the sacraments are not equally fruitful in everyone who receives them. While everyone at Mass may receive the Body and Blood of Christ, the fruitfulness of this sacramental communion will vary. This is because "the fruits of the sacraments also depend on the disposition of the one who receives them" (CCC, 1128). The most obvious example is when someone receives a sacrament in a state of mortal sin, but other dispositions such as indifference or a lack of faith can also limit the fruitfulness of sacramental grace. This was true during Jesus's earthly ministry. When he went to Nazareth, his hometown, the people "took offense at him. . . . And he

---

21. Johann Auer, *A General Doctrine of the Sacraments and the Mystery of The Eucharist* (Washington, DC: The Catholic University of America Press, 1995), 49.

22. Ibid.

23. Paul Haffner, *The Sacramental Mystery*, rev. ed. (Herefordshire: Gracewing, 2007), 21.

24. Ibid., 22.

did not work many mighty deeds there because of their lack of faith" (Mt 13:57–58). On the other hand, Jesus praised the Canaanite woman who asked him to heal her daughter: "'O woman, great is your faith! Let it be done for you as you wish.' And her daughter was healed from that hour" (Mt 15:28). There is an intimate and reciprocal relationship between the sacraments and faith: "They not only presuppose faith, but by words and objects they also nourish, strengthen, and express it. That is why they are called 'sacraments *of faith*'" (CCC, 1123). Through the sacraments God imparts his help and life to us, but we must prepare ourselves to receive them with faith and humility.

TRANSFORMATION OF LIFE

As an example of the transforming power of the sacraments, let us look at the Sacrament of Confirmation. In addition to the sacramental rite, the biblical readings, the Church Fathers, and the *Catechism*, there is a fifth source of information about each sacrament: the orations (prayers) for the ritual Mass for the celebration of each of the sacraments (with the exception of the Sacrament of Reconciliation). For example, the ritual Mass for the conferral of Confirmation has two sets of prayers for the Collect (opening prayer), the Prayer over the Gifts, and the Prayer after Communion. Let us now look at the second set of prayers (B) to see what they reveal about the meaning of Confirmation for the whole of one's life.

We shall begin with the opening prayer, known as the Collect since it "collects" the prayers of the gathered assembly and offers them to the Father.

> Graciously pour out your Holy Spirit upon us,
> we pray, O Lord,
> so that, walking in oneness of faith
> and strengthened by the power of his love,
> we may come to the measure of the full stature of Christ.[25]

This prayer reveals several transforming aspects of the Sacrament of Confirmation. It begins by imploring the gift of the Spirit which is the essential grace of the sacrament: "Graciously pour out your Holy Spirit upon us." It then enumerates three lifelong fruits. The first is

---

25. *Roman Missal*, Ritual Mass for the Conferral of Confirmation, Collect B.

working for the unity of all believers: "walking in oneness of faith." Jesus prayed for this unity in his high priestly prayer recorded in John 17: "I pray not only for them, but also for those who will believe in me through their word, so that they may all be one, as you, Father, are in me and I in you, that they also may be in us, that the world may believe that you sent me" (Jn 17:20–21). The second fruit is being strengthened by God's love, which according to St. Paul's Letter to the Romans is a specific gift of the Spirit: "the love of God has been poured into our hearts through the holy Spirit that has been given to us" (Rom 5:5). The third fruit is being conformed to the image of Christ: "we may come to the measure of the full stature of Christ." This petition is taken from the Letter to the Ephesians in which St. Paul speaks of the "building up of the body Christ, until we all attain to the unity of faith and knowledge of the Son of God, to mature manhood, to the extent of the full stature of Christ" (4:12–13). This brief but rich prayer expresses both the personal and the ecclesial effects of the sacrament: through the gift of the Spirit the recipient is strengthened by Christ's love and progressively conformed to his image so as to work for the unity of all believers so that together they may come to "the full stature of Christ."

The second prayer is the Prayer over the Gifts, offered in response to the congregation's petition that the Lord would accept the sacrifice at the priest's hands "for the praise and glory of his name, for our good, and the good of all his holy Church" (RM, Order of Mass, 29):

> Accept graciously these your servants, O Lord,
> together with your Only Begotten Son,
> so that, signed with his Cross and with a spiritual anointing,
> they may constantly offer themselves to you
> in union with him
> and merit each day a greater outpouring of your Spirit.[26]

This prayer begins by making reference to the essential signs of the Sacrament of Confirmation: "signed with his Cross and with a spiritual anointing." It then speaks of two specific transformative fruits. The first is a continual offering of oneself to the Father in union with Christ. This is the character of filial love, to offer oneself to God for the sake of others. The second fruit is a continued outpouring of the Spirit, for God "does not ration

---

26. *Roman Missal*, Ritual Mass for the Conferral of Confirmation, Prayer over the Offerings B.

his gift of the Spirit" (Jn 3:34). As with the collect, we see here both a personal dimension—an ever-greater outpouring of the Spirit—and an ecclesial dimension—the filial offering of oneself with Christ for the Church and the world.

The final prayer is the Prayer after Communion. Since it is proclaimed following the reception of sacramental communion, this prayer focuses on the fruits that flow from the reception of the Body and Blood of the Lord.

> Instruct, O Lord, in the fullness of the Law
> those you have endowed with the gifts of your Spirit
> and nourished by the Body of your Only Begotten Son,
> that they may constantly show to the world
> the freedom of your adopted children
> and, by the holiness of their lives,
> exercise the prophetic mission of your people. [27]

This prayer begins by affirming the relationship between Confirmation, which endows the recipient "with the gifts of your Spirit," and the Eucharist, which nourishes the recipient with "the Body of your Only Begotten Son."

The Eucharist contains "the entire spiritual wealth of the church, namely Christ himself our Pasch and our living bread, who gives life to humanity through his flesh," and so all of the sacraments "are bound up with the Eucharist and are directed towards it" (PO, 5). This is especially true of the sacraments of initiation: "It must never be forgotten that our reception of Baptism and Confirmation is ordered to the Eucharist" (SacCar, 17). Thus transformed, those confirmed become signs to the world of the freedom of the children of God. Finally, the holiness made possible by the gifts of the Spirit enable the confirmed to participate in the prophetic mission of the Church, for "the gifts of the Spirit are given for the building up of Christ's Body (1 Cor 12) and for ever greater witness to the Gospel in the world" (SacCar 17). Again we see both personal and ecclesial effects: personal holiness and freedom which make believers signs to the world and prophetic witnesses to the world, if we are aware of and act with the graces we have received.

---

27. *Roman Missal*, Ritual Mass for the Conferral of Confirmation, Prayer after Communion B.

These prayers for the Mass for the Conferral of Confirmation contain a rich theology of the transforming power of the Sacrament of Confirmation. They indicate the different ways that one's entire life is progressively transformed by the sacrament: strengthened by God's love, increasingly conformed to the image of Christ, filled more and more with the Spirit, and walking in holiness. This personal transformation expresses itself through participation in the mission of the Church, the Body of Christ: working for the unity of all believers, offering oneself to God with Christ for others, becoming ever more transparent living signs to the world of freedom in Christ, and offering a prophetic witness to the world.

CONCLUSION

In its *Constitution on the Sacred Liturgy*, the Second Vatican Council put special emphasis on "full, conscious, and active participation in liturgical celebrations" by all the faithful (SC, 14). "In the reform and promotion of the liturgy, this full and active participation by all the people is *the aim to be considered before all else*" (SC, 14; italics added). The Council's vision of participation has two dimensions, interior and exterior. Interior participation requires "a good understanding of the rites and prayers" so all present are "conscious of what they are doing, with devotion and full involvement" (SC, 48). Exterior participation means participating "by means of acclamations, responses, psalmody, antiphons, and songs, as well as by actions, gestures, and bearing. And at the proper times all should observe a reverent silence" (SC, 30). It also means that those who have a role to perform, whether minister or layperson, "should do all of, but only, those parts" proper to their office (SC, 28). The Church urges this full, conscious, and active participation because "it is the primary and indispensable source from which the faithful are to derive the true Christian spirit" (SC, 14).

The method of mystagogical catechesis proposed by Pope Benedict XVI and illustrated in this chapter can facilitate the kind of interior and exterior participation envisioned by the Church. Looking at the Old Testament roots of a sacrament reveals the unity of God's revelation in word and deed, a revelation that finds its fulfillment in Christ. Understanding the meaning of the liturgical signs, which carry within them the saving power of Christ's Paschal Mystery, enables us to pass from the signs to the mysteries they contain and to encounter Christ, who is the meaning of all of the signs. This in turn opens us up to the transforming power of each sacrament so that we may know the love of Christ which surpasses knowledge and adore the one who "is able to accomplish far more than all we ask or imagine" (Eph 3:20).

PART II

The Sacrament of Penance and Reconciliation

The call to conversion is an integral part of the proclamation of the Kingdom of God: "The time is fulfilled, and the kingdom of God is at hand; repent, and believe in the gospel" (CCC, 1427). "Baptism is the principal place for the first and fundamental conversion" (CCC, 1427).[1] However, God calls us to conversion throughout our lives. "This *second conversion* is an uninterrupted task for the whole Church. . . . It is the movement of a 'contrite heart,' drawn and moved by grace to respond to the merciful love of God who loved us first" (CCC, 1428). In this section we will look at the Sacrament of Penance through which Christ continues to touch us through the power of the Holy Spirit and to assist us in "the struggle of conversion directed toward holiness and eternal life to which the Lord never ceases to call us" (CCC, 1426).

The struggle of conversion is particularly challenging in our time. Pius XII stated that "the sin of the century is the loss of the sense of sin,"[2] an observation echoed by his successors. Pope Bl. Paul VI observed in 1972, "Ours is an age that desperately needs to recover a clear, well-founded moral consciousness and that yearns for liberation from the force that

---

1. The *Catechism* qualifies Baptism as the "principal place" for the first conversion because the Church recognizes the possibility of salvation for those who do not receive the sacrament due to martyrdom, sudden death, or circumstances: "Those who die for the faith, those who are catechumens [those who are preparing for baptism], and all those who, without knowing of the Church but acting under the inspiration of grace, seek God sincerely and strive to fulfill his will, can be saved even if they have not been baptized" (CCC, 1281).

2. Pope Pius XII, Radio Message to the US National Catechetical Congress in Boston (October 26,1946), *Discorsi e Radiomessaggi* VIII (1946): 288.

most interiorly and oppressively holds people prisoner."[3] St. John Paul II in *Reconciliation and Penance* quoted this assertion by Pope Pius XII, describing them as "words that have almost become proverbial" (RaP, 18) and stated in the strongest terms, "The sacrament of penance is in crisis" (RaP, 28). At the close of the Great Jubilee Year of 2000, 17 years later, he again acknowledged "the crisis of 'the sense of sin' in today's culture" and proposed to the universal Church as a pastoral priority encouraging "persuasively and effectively" the Sacrament of Reconciliation.[4]

St. John Paul II has not only noted the crisis of the sense of sin and its effect on the Sacrament of Penance but has discussed at length various factors that have contributed to this crisis (RaP, 18). He begins by looking at four social-cultural factors that contribute to this loss of the sense of sin. First, he notes the influence of a secularism that emphasizes production, consumerism, and pleasure seeking and reduces sin to anything that offends man. Teachings that place the blame for sin upon society or the influences of environment and historical conditioning and declare the individual free of all responsibility are a second factor. Added to this is a denial that certain actions or attitudes are always wrong and sinful—to some people everything is relative, there are no absolutes. Finally, he notes a false identification of sin with "a morbid feeling of guilt or with the mere transgression of legal norms and precepts"—breaking the rules rather than hurting a relationship rooted in love.

In addition to these factors, St. John Paul II also acknowledges certain trends in the thought and life the Church that "inevitably favor the decline of the sense of sin" (RaP, 18). In some cases, he observes, a tendency to see sin everywhere has been replaced by a failure to recognize it anywhere. Also, an exaggerated emphasis on the fear of eternal punishment has given way "to preaching a love of God that excludes any punishment deserved by sin" (RaP, 18). Finally, some have passed "from severity in trying to correct erroneous consciences . . . to a kind of respect for conscience which excludes the duty of telling the truth" (RaP, 18).

A third set of factors noted by the saint concern sacramental practice. Sin has both an individual and a communal dimension—it wounds our

---

3. Paul VI, Address to a General Audience, "On the Sacrament of Reconciliation," July 19, 1972, *Not* 8 (1972): 305–307, in *Documents on the Liturgy* [DOL], n. 363, p. 954.

4. John Paul II, *Novo Millennio Ineunte* (Boston: Pauline Books and Media, 2001), n. 37.

relationship with God, and it hurts our relationship with others and the Church. Today, notes the saint, there is "the tendency to obscure the ecclesial significance of sin and of conversion and to reduce them to merely personal matters; or vice versa, the tendency to nullify the personal value of good and evil and to consider only their community dimension" (RaP, 18). Finally, he notes "the danger, never totally eliminated, of routine ritualism that deprives the sacrament of its full significance and formative effectiveness" (RaP, 18). What is needed, he says, is "a rediscovery of Christ as . . . the one in whom God shows us his compassionate heart and reconciles us fully with himself. It is this face of Christ that must be rediscovered through the Sacrament of Penance."[5]

In chapter 4 we will begin with an overview of the Sacrament of Penance. Then we will examine several Old Testament passages that prefigure the sacrament in different ways. We first look at David's sin with Bathsheba, his repentance and conversion, and his intense expression of contrition in Psalm 51. We will next study God's call to Israel to repent through the prophet Jeremiah. The third passage we will examine is God's promise of a new heart and a new spirit through the prophet Ezekiel. Finally, we will look at an Old Testament communal penance service from the book of Nehemiah.

The sacramental signs and symbols which comprise the Sacrament of Penance and Reconciliation are the subject of chapter 5. We will look at the key acts of the penitent: the examination of conscience, contrition, confession, and satisfaction of the penitent; and the essential words of the priest—the formula of absolution and the accompanying gestures. The participants themselves, not only the penitent and priest but also the community, are also sacramental signs. Lastly we will look at the different forms of celebration and the spiritual realities that they signify.

We will conclude part 2 with a presentation in chapter 6 of the transforming power of the sacrament in our lives. The fundamental effect of this sacrament is reconciliation with God, but this reconciliation then leads to other reconciliations, with the Church and within one's own heart. The grace of the sacrament also confers peace and consolation as well as strength for spiritual battle. We will also look at the eternal and temporal

---

5. Ibid

punishments for sin and the doctrine of indulgences. We will conclude with the final reconciliation, reconciliation with all creation.

In preparation for this study of the Sacrament of Penance, let us listen to Pope Bl. Paul VI's exhortation from 1972, words that continue to encourage us today: "We address ourselves to you, our brothers in the priesthood, called to be physicians of souls, confidants, masters, psychiatrists of grace, in the extremely effective and at the same time delicate and grave ministry of confession. We address ourself to all of you, the faithful sons and daughters of the Church, both to those who have the happy experience of his sacrament and to those who may have been held back from it by a deep-rooted pride or by groundless fears. We exhort all of you to have esteem, reverence, gratitude, and desire for this 'ministry of reconciliation' (2 Cor 5:18), which truly means the paschal joy of resurrection."[6]

---

6. Paul VI, DOL, n. 365.

Chapter 4

Penance and Reconciliation: An Overview and Old Testament Roots

The psalms give eloquent voice to the pain and burden of sin.

> There is no wholesomeness in my flesh because of your anger;
> there is no health in my bones because of my sin.
> My iniquities overwhelm me,
> a burden too heavy for me.
> Foul and festering are my sores
> because of my folly.
> I am stooped and deeply bowed;
> every day I go about mourning.
> My loins burn with fever;
> there is no wholesomeness in my flesh.
> I am numb and utterly crushed;
> I wail with anguish of heart. (Ps 38:4–9)

The psalmist's entire existence is transfigured by his sin, for his suffering is both physical and spiritual. The destructive power of unconfessed sin is also vividly acknowledged:

> Because I kept silent, my bones wasted away;
> I groaned all day long.
> For day and night your hand was heavy upon me;
> my strength withered as in dry summer heat.
> Then I declared my sin to you;
> my guilt I did not hide.
> I said, "I confess my transgression to the LORD,"
> and you took away the guilt of my sin. (Ps 32:3–5)

These psalms express in powerful and vivid language the profound anguish of sin.

RICH IN MERCY

The sinner's anguished cry has not gone unheard. God, "who is rich in mercy" (Eph 2:4), has heard this anguished cry of his people and in Christ has come to their aid. Not only did Christ call people to repentance and welcome sinners, "he himself died for our sins and rose again for our justification" (RP, 1). The Lord has provided three remedies for sin through his body, the Church. The first remedy for sin is Baptism, "where our fallen nature is crucified with Christ so that the body of sin may be destroyed and we may no longer be slaves to sin, but rise with Christ and live for God. For this reason the Church proclaims its faith in 'the one baptism for the forgiveness of sins'" (RP, 2). The second remedy for sin is the Eucharist, for at the Last Supper "he instituted the sacrifice of the new covenant in his blood for the forgiveness of sins" (RP, 1). The Eucharist "is a remedy to free us from our daily faults and to preserve us from mortal sins" (CCC, 1536). It strengthens and nourishes believers in conversion and holiness.

The third remedy is the Sacrament of Penance and Reconciliation. "Christ instituted the Sacrament of Penance for all sinful members of his Church," especially for those who, since their Baptism, have fallen into grave sin. The Fathers of the Church described this sacrament as "the second plank [of salvation] after the shipwreck which is the loss of grace" (CCC, 1446). The Church, wrote St. Ambrose (d. 397), "possesses both water and tears: the water of baptism, the tears of penance" (RP, 2). The mercy of God manifested in Christ is infinite. "Also infinite therefore and inexhaustible is the Father's readiness to receive the prodigal children who return to His home. Infinite are the readiness and power of forgiveness which flow continually from the marvelous value of the sacrifice of the Son. No human sin can prevail over this power or even limit it. On the part of man only a lack of good will can limit it, a lack of readiness to be converted and to repent, in other words persistence in obstinacy, opposing grace and truth, especially in the face of the witness of the cross and resurrection of Christ" (DiM, 13).

The Church recognizes two dimensions of sin, personal and communal. On the personal level it is "an offense against God, a rupture of communion with him" (CCC, 1440). Sin damages our personal relationship with God. But sin also has a communal dimension, because "it damages communion with the Church" (CCC, 1440). "Sin," wrote Pope

Benedict XVI, "is never a purely individual affair; it always damages the ecclesial communion that we have entered through Baptism" (SacCar, 20). Both aspects must be healed. "For this reason conversion entails both God's forgiveness and reconciliation with the Church, which are expressed and accomplished liturgically by the sacrament of Penance and Reconciliation" (CCC, 1440).

The Church Fathers stressed the healing character of penance and forgiveness. In the fourth century St. Basil the Great (d. 379) compared confession to physical healing: "In the confession of sins, the same order is to be observed that is applied in disclosing illnesses of the body. Accordingly, just as men do not lay open their bodily illness to all, nor to anyone, but to those who are skillful in the healing of them, so too the confession of sins ought to be made before those who can heal them."[1] A few decades later, Theodore of Mopsuestia (d. 428) described priests as "physicians of sins" who administered the "medicine of repentance": "Since you are aware . . . of the fact that because God greatly care for us He gave us penitence and showed us the medicine of repentance, and established some men, who are priests, as physicians of sins, so that if we receive in this world through them healing and forgiveness of sins, we shall be delivered from the judgment to come—it behooves us to draw nigh unto the priests with great confidence and to reveal our sins to them, and they, with all diligence, pain, and love . . . will give healing to sinners. And they will not disclose the things that are not to be disclosed, but they will keep to themselves the things that have happened, as fits true and loving fathers, bound to safeguard the shame of their children while striving to heal their bodies."[2] St. Augustine summed up the healing character of this sacrament: "I wish to heal, not accuse" (RaP, 31.II).

In addition to its healing character, the Sacrament of Penance and Reconciliation also has the character of judgment. In the sacrament, "sinners reveal their sins and their condition as creatures subject to sin; they commit themselves to renouncing and combating sin; accept the punishment (sacramental penance) which the confessor imposes on them and receive absolution from him" (RaP, 31.II). However, this judgment is made in the depths of God's mercy. "According to the most

---

1. Monti, *A Sense of the Sacred*, 136.
2. Ibid., 137.

ancient traditional idea, the sacrament is a kind of judicial action; but this takes place before a tribunal of mercy rather than of strict and rigorous justice" (RaP, 31.II). For this reason, the Church recognizes "over and above the character of judgment in the sense just mentioned a healing of a medicinal character. And this is linked to the fact that the Gospel frequently presents Christ as healer (Lk 5:31f.; 9:2), while his redemptive work is often called, from Christian antiquity, *medicina salutis* [medicine of health]" (RaP, 31.II). The *Rite of Penance* describes the act of penance (satisfaction) as a "remedy" by which the penitent is "cured of the sickness from which he suffered" (RP, 6c). "God never tires of forgiving us," writes Pope Francis, "we are the ones who tire of seeking his mercy. . . . No one can strip us of the dignity bestowed upon us by this boundless and unfailing love" (EG, 3).

THE SACRAMENT OF PENANCE AND RECONCILIATION

The different names for this sacrament—conversion, confession, forgiveness, Reconciliation, Penance—reveal its various facets and power. It is the sacrament of conversion "because it makes sacramentally present Jesus' call to conversion, the first step in returning to the Father from whom one has strayed by sin" (CCC, 1423). It is called the sacrament of confession, "since the disclosure or confession of sins to a priest is an essential element of this sacrament" (CCC, 1424). It is also a confession in the broader sense of the word, the "acknowledgment and praise of the holiness of God and of his mercy toward sinful man" (CCC, 1424). Because God grants to the penitent "pardon and peace" through the priest's sacrament absolution, it is also called the sacrament of forgiveness (CCC, 1424). It is also known as the Sacrament of Reconciliation "because it imparts to the sinner the life of God who reconciles" and enables him or her "to respond to the Lord's call: 'Go; first be reconciled to your brother' (Mt 5:24)" (CCC, 1424). Finally, "It is called the sacrament of Penance, since it consecrates the Christian sinner's personal and ecclesial steps of conversion, penance, and satisfaction" (CCC, 1423). This is the title of the official ritual book, the *Rite of Penance*. The *Catechism of the Catholic Church* refers to it as the Sacrament of Penance and Reconciliation.

SIN

The *Catechism* defines sin as "a deliberate thought, word, deed, or omission contrary to the eternal law of God" (CCC, glossary). This is what we confess in the Mass: "I have greatly sinned, in my thoughts and in my words, in what I have done and in what I have failed to do" (RM, Order of Mass, 4). To prepare for the Sacrament of Penance and Reconciliation it is important to examine our consciences and consider the seriousness of our sins, evaluating our sins "according to their gravity" (CCC, 1854). In doing so, "it is customary to distinguish between mortal and venial sins" (CCC, glossary). This distinction is based on 1 John 5:16–17:

> If anyone sees his brother sinning, if the sin is not deadly,
> > he should pray to God
> and he will give him life. This is only for those
> whose sin is not deadly.
> There is such a thing as deadly sin, about which
> > I do not say that you should pray.
> All wrongdoing is sin, but there is sin that is not deadly.

In this passage, John distinguishes between sins that are "deadly" and sins that are "not deadly." The tradition of the Church calls deadly sin mortal sin, and sin that is not deadly venial sin. Mortal sin is "a grave infraction of the law of God that destroys the divine life in the soul of the sinner (sanctifying grace), constituting a turn away from God. Venial sin wounds but "does not destroy the divine life in the soul" (CCC, glossary).

However, the *Rite of Penance* uses somewhat different language. It still talks about venial sin, which is the result of "daily weakness" and a failure to gain "the full freedom of the children of God" (RP, 7). But instead of *mortal* sin, it speaks of *grave* sin, which it describes as a withdrawal "from the communion of love with God" (RP, 7). For a sin to be mortal or grave, three conditions must be present: it must be grave or serious matter, the sinner must know that it is grave matter, and he or she must freely choose to commit the sin. Only when these three conditions are present can one be *held responsible* for committing a grave sin. In assessing this responsibility for grave sin, Pope Francis reminds us of the Church's teaching that one's *responsibility* for a sinful action, which *in and of itself* is grave, is affected by other factors: "pastors and the lay faithful who accompany their brothers and sisters in faith or on a journey of openness to God must always remember what the *Catechism of the Catholic Church* teaches quite clearly: 'Imputability and responsibility for an action can be diminished or even nullified by ignorance, inadvertence, duress, fear, habit, inordinate attachments, and other psychological or social factors' (CCC, 1735)" (EG, 44). God wants us to enter into the love of the Trinity and so live in full freedom as his children—sin is a rejection of God's desire to bring us into a communion of love and freedom.

THE MINISTER AND SEAL OF THE SACRAMENT

Christ entrusted the ministry of reconciliation to his Apostles (Jn 20:23). Their successors, bishops, and priests who are their collaborators, continue Christ's reconciling work. "The competent minister of the sacrament of penance is a priest who has the faculty to absolve" (RP, 9b). "It suffices," wrote Pope St. Leo the Great in the fifth century, "for the guilt of consciences to be made known only to the priests in secret confession."[3] The Church, recognizing "the delicacy and greatness of this ministry and the respect due to persons" (CCC, 1467), binds every confessor "under very severe penalties to keep absolute secrecy regarding the sins his penitents have confessed to him. He can make no use of knowledge that confession gives him about penitents' lives" (CCC, 1467). There are no exceptions to this secret, called the "sacramental seal," because the penitent's confession is "'sealed' by the sacrament" (CCC, 1467). This seal "indicates that the penitential celebration of the sacrament is a reality of grace whose *iter* [method] is already 'traced out' in the Heart of Jesus and in deep friendship with him. Once again, the mystery and dignity of man are made manifest in the mystery of Christ" (PMDM, 32).

THE PLACE FOR CONFESSIONS

The ordinary place for the celebration of the sacrament, "except for a legitimate reason," is a confessional (RP, 12). The American bishops have further stipulated that the confessional "be visible and accessible, that it contain a fixed grille, and that it allow for confession face-to-face

---

3. Monti, *A Sense of the Sacred,* 48.

for those who wish to do so."[4] The importance of the placement, design and furnishings of the confessional should not be underestimated, for these features "can assist penitents on the path to contrition and sorrow for sin and to proclaim their reconciliation with God and the community of faith."[5]

CELEBRATING THE RITE OF PENANCE AND RECONCILIATION

Although the sacrament has, over the centuries, undergone changes in its discipline and celebration, it has preserved a fundamental structure consisting of two essential elements, the acts of the penitent and the action of God mediated through the Church. The acts of the penitent are the first essential element: contrition, or sorrow and hatred for sin "together with a resolution not to sin again" (CCC, glossary); confession, "telling one's sins to the priestly minister" (CCC, glossary); and satisfaction, "an act whereby the sinner makes amends for sin, especially in reparation to God for offenses against him" (CCC, glossary). The action of God through the intervention of the Church constitutes the second essential element. In the name of Jesus Christ the bishop and his priests forgive sins, determine the manner of satisfaction (the penance), pray for the sinner, and do penance with him (CCC, 1448). "Thus the sinner is healed and re-established in ecclesial communion" (CCC, 1448).

The *Rite of Penance* provides two forms for the ordinary celebration of the sacrament: a rite for the reconciliation of individual penitents and a rite for the reconciliation of several penitents with individual confession and absolution (often celebrated during Advent and Lent). Both forms have the same basic structure. They begin with introductory rites followed by a liturgy of the word, the celebration of the sacrament (confession, satisfaction, contrition, and absolution), concluding with praise and proclamation of God's mercy. As the chart below indicates, the introductory rites, liturgy of the word, and concluding rites are elaborated in the communal celebration.

---

4. United States Conference of Catholic Bishops, *Built of Living Stones: Art, Architecture and Worship* (Washington, DC: USCCB Publishing, 2000), 103.

5. Ibid., 104.

Reconciliation of Individual Penitents	*Reconciliation of Several Penitents with Individual Confession and Absolution*
Reception of Penitent	Introductory Rites
Greeting	Song
Sign of the Cross	Greeting
Invitation to Trust in God	Introduction
	Opening Prayer
Reading of the Word of God	Celebration of the Word of God
	First Reading
	Responsorial Psalm
	Second Readingw
	Gospel Acclamation
	Gospel
	Homily
	Examination of Conscience
Confession of Sins and Acceptance of Satisfaction	Rite of Reconciliation
	General Confession of Sin
	Litany or Song
	Lord's Prayer
	Individual Confession
Prayer of the Penitent and Absolution	Absolution
Proclamation of Praise of God and Dismissal	Proclamation of Praise for God's Mercy
	Concluding Prayer of Thanksgiving
	Concluding Rite
	Blessing
	Dismissal

A third form is the Rite for Reconciliation of Penitents with General Confession and Absolution. This, however, is only to be used in extreme and specific circumstances: when the "danger of death is imminent" (31a) or when "a serious need is present" (31b). Finally, Appendix II of the *Rite of Penance* provides a number of model liturgies: for the seasons of Lent and Advent; on themes such as sin and conversion, the prodigal's return, and the beatitudes; and for different groups, including children, young people, and the sick.

Whichever form is celebrated, "The celebration of the sacrament is essentially liturgical, festive and joyful in that, guided by the Holy Spirit, it is oriented towards re-encounter with God and with the Good Shepherd" (PMDM, 25).

THE WORD OF GOD IN THE SACRAMENT OF PENANCE AND RECONCILIATION

Pope Benedict XVI stressed the importance of Sacred Scripture in celebrating the Sacrament of Penance.

> We ought never to forget that "the word of God is a word of reconciliation, for in it God has reconciled all things to himself (cf. 2 Cor 5:18–20; Eph 1:10). The loving forgiveness of God, made flesh in Jesus, raises up the sinner." (VD, 61) "Through the word of God the Christian receives light to recognize his sins and is called to conversion and to confidence in God's mercy" (RP, 17).

He suggests various ways in which the sacred Scriptures can heighten the power of the sacrament:

> To have a deeper experience of the reconciling power of God's word, the individual penitent should be encouraged to prepare for confession by meditating on a suitable text of sacred Scripture and to begin confession by reading or listening to a biblical exhortation such as those provided in the rite. When expressing contrition it would be good if the penitent were to use "prayer based on the words of Scripture," (RP, 19) such as those indicated in the rite. When possible, it would be good that at particular times of the year, or whenever the opportunity presents itself, individual confession by a number of penitents should take place within penitential celebrations as provided for by the ritual, with due respect for the different liturgical traditions; here greater time can be devoted to the celebration of the word through the use of suitable readings. (VD, 61)

The *Rite of Penance* recommends readings that focus on three different aspects of the sacrament, God's call to conversion "and ever closer conformity with Christ," reconciliation as a fruit of Christ's Paschal Mystery "through the gift of the Holy Spirit," and assistance in examining one's conscience (RP, 24b). The RP includes a large number of suggested passages from the Old and New Testaments, but it permits other choices as well: "For diversity, and according to the nature of the group, other readings may be selected" (RP, rubric for 101–201). In this book, we will look at passages recommend by the RP.

I HAVE SINNED AGAINST THE LORD: 2 SAMUEL 12:1–9, 13

If there is a paradigmatic Old Testament passage foreshadowing the Sacrament of Penance and Reconciliation, it is David's sin with Bathsheba. The story is a familiar one. On a spring evening, David—now the king of Israel—sees Bathsheba, wife of Uriah the Hittite, Joab's armor bearer, bathing. He sends for her, and they conceive a child. When David learns that she is pregnant, he tries to cover up his role by arranging for Uriah to return home, hoping that he will be seen as the father. However, Uriah refuses to go to his own home and instead sleeps at the entrance to the king's house. Thwarted in his first attempt at a cover-up, David then arranges Uriah's death, ordering the commanders to place Uriah at the front of the battle, and then have the rest of the soldiers pull back, leaving Uriah alone and exposed. And so it happens—Uriah is killed in battle. David, following the accepted period of mourning, marries Bathsheba, and she gives birth to their son.

The passage from the RP—2 Samuel 12:1–9, 13—takes up the story at this point. The Lord sends Nathan, the court prophet, to David with a story of two men, one rich, one poor. The rich man owned great flocks and herds, but the poor man had only one ewe lamb which he tenderly cared for so that "she was like a daughter to him" (12:3). When the rich man wanted to prepare a meal for a visitor, he took the poor man's ewe lamb rather than a lamb for his own flocks. At this point in Nathan's story, David, indignant at the rich man's actions, exclaims, "As the LORD lives, the man who has done this merits death! He shall restore the ewe lamb fourfold because he has done this and has had no pity." Nathan replies, "You are the man!" (12:6–7). He then delivers the Lord's word to David, reminding him of the way God has blessed him, and then recounting his sin. David replies, "I have sinned against the LORD." Nathan then tells David, "The LORD on his part has forgiven your sin: you shall not die" (12:13).

This event reveals several important aspects of the Sacrament of Penance. It involves grave sins—adultery and murder. We also see David's blindness to his sin—he does not recognized it until Nathan's dramatic words, "You are the man." This also illustrates the power of God's word to break through the sinner's blindness and hard-heartedness, exemplifying the words of Pope Benedict XVI, "Through the word of God the Christian receives light to recognize his sins and is called to conversion and to confidence in God's mercy" (VD, 61). It is the Lord's word proclaimed through the prophet Nathan that brings David to recognition and conversion. David's acknowledgement of his sin—"I have sinned against the Lord"—prefigures the confession of sin. Finally, forgiveness is declared through the Lord's representative, in this case the prophet Nathan.

St. John Paul II summarizes the meaning of this passage for the Church's understanding of Penance. The sacrament's "point of departure is the church's conviction that man, to whom every form of pastoral activity is directed but principally that of penance and reconciliation, is the man marked by sin whose striking image is to be found in King David. Rebuked by the prophet Nathan, David faces squarely his own iniquity and confesses: 'I have sinned against the Lord,' (12:13) and proclaims: 'I know my transgressions, and my sin is ever before me' (Ps 51:3). But he also prays: 'Purge me with hyssop, and I shall be clean; wash me, and I shall be whiter than snow,' (Ps 51:7) and he receives the response of the divine mercy: 'The Lord has put away your sin; you shall not die'" (12:13) (RaP, 23). He continues, "The church thus finds herself face to face with man—with the whole human world—wounded by sin and affected by sin in the innermost depths of his being. But at the same time he is moved by an unrestrainable desire to be freed from sin and, especially if he is a Christian, he is aware that the mystery of *pietas* [piety or mercy], Christ the Lord, is already acting in him and in the world by the power of the redemption" (RaP, 23).

Reflecting on this tragic event in David's life, we may be puzzled by one of the biblical descriptions of David, that he was a man after God's own heart (1 Sam 13:14; Acts 13:22, et al.). How, we may wonder, is an adulterer and murderer a man after God's own heart? The very event that poses this question provides us with the answer. He was not a man after God's own heart because he lived a perfect, sinless life. Rather, I suspect, it is because of the tenderness of his heart when he was confronted with his sin. He did not argue, defend, or make excuses—unlike his ancestors, Adam and Eve—but frankly and humbly acknowledged his sin and sought the Lord's forgiveness. Then he began again, illustrating the words of St. Paul: "Just one thing: forgetting what lies behind but straining forward to what lies ahead, I continue my pursuit toward the goal, the prize of God's upward calling, in Christ Jesus" (Phil 3:14).

HAVE MERCY ON ME: PSALM 51:3–14, 17, 19

St. John Paul II, in his discussion of David's sin with Bathsheba quoted above, cites not only the historical narrative in 2 Samuel but also Psalm 51, a psalm that is attributed to David "when Nathan the prophet came to him after he had gone in to Bathsheba" (51:2).[6] Psalm 51:3–14, 17, 19 is one of the options in the RP for the Responsorial Psalm. Psalm 51 is one of the seven penitential psalms; the others are Psalms 6, 32, 38, 102, 130, and 143, three of which, Psalms 32, 130, and 143, are also options in the RP. The description and grouping of these seven psalms goes back to the Middle Ages. "These psalms were originally recited at the deathbed or sickbed of a person for recovery of health or forgiveness in death. Later they were associated with the life of David, which extended their use in the church."[7]

The psalm begins with a cry for deliverance: "Have mercy on me . . . wipe out my offense. Thoroughly wash me from my guilt and of my sin cleanse me" (vv. 3–4). David appeals not to his own merits but to God's mercy and the greatness of his compassion (v. 3). He feels intensely the offense of his sin: "Against you only have I sinned, and done what is evil in your sight" (v. 6). Guilt is not just a personal feeling "but has an objective reference; it is an act against someone outside the self, against the Holy God. No act of self-deception or any cover-up can deal with sin in this radical sense."[8] "Sin," explains the *Catechism* citing this verse, "sets itself against God's love for us and turns our hearts away from it" (CCC, 1850). God, who is "pleased with sincerity of heart," is the one who has enabled him to see his sin: "in my inmost

---

6. In some translations, this heading of the psalm, including the version in the RP, is numbered verses 1 and 2, so that the first verse of the psalm—"Have mercy on me, O God, in your goodness . . . "—is verse 3. In other translations, including St. John Paul II's references, the heading is not numbered, so that "Have mercy on me, O God, in your goodness . . . " is verse 1. Thus the verse "Purge me with hyssop . . . " is v. 7 in John Paul II's reference and v. 9 in the NABRE.

7. Bernhard W. Anderson with Steven Bishop, *Out of the Depths: The Psalms Speak for Us Today* (Louisville, KY: Westminster John Knox Press, 2000), 78.

8. Ibid., 82.

being you teach me wisdom" (v. 8). He prays for "the kind of *discernment* that will make a new, responsible life possible."[9]

Following this sincere and sorrowful confession of his sin, David implores forgiveness and healing—"cleanse me . . . wash me. . . . Turn away your face from my sins, and blot out all my guilt" (vv. 9, 11). Even more, he asks the Lord to give him a clean heart and to renew a steadfast spirit (v. 10). His request that God create a clean heart merits closer examination. The Hebrew word here for heart "refers to the mind and the will, that is, the center of the self from which action and loyalty spring. 'The heart has its reasons,' said the French writer Pascal (1623–1662), 'of which [abstract] reason does not know.'"[10] The Hebrew verb that is translated "create"—*bara*—"is used in the Old Testament only of God's action, the classic example being the Genesis creation story (cf. also Isa 45:12)."[11] In addition, "the prayer for a 'steadfast sprit' (NJPS) is reminiscent of the second story of creation where God is portrayed breathing into clay the divine spirit (*ruach*) which gives vitality to the self (*nefesh*). Here we find the amazing testimony that God's forgiveness may animate the body with new breath, with the 'holy spirit' that gives new vitality."[12]

The psalm refers also to liturgical worship, including ritual washing (v. 20)—"thoroughly wash me from my guilt"—and purification with hyssop (v. 9)—"Cleanse me of sin with hyssop, that I may be purified." Hyssop is "a small bush whose many wood twigs make a natural sprinkler. It was prescribed in the Mosaic law as an instrument for sprinkling sacrificial blood or lustral water for cleansing, cf. Ex 12:22; Lv 14:4; Num 19:18."[13] These formal acts of worship, however, "signify nothing unless they are outward expressions of an inward relationship to God. On the other hand, God may use the cultic forms of worship to bring about a new life of health and wholeness (the meaning of 'peace,' shalom)."[14]

---

9. Walter Brueggemann, *Message of Psalms: A Theological Commentary* (Minneapolis: Fortress Press, 1985), 100.

10. Anderson, *Out of the Depths*, 82.

11. Ibid.

12. Ibid., 83.

13. *New American Bible*, rev. St. Joseph medium size ed. (New Jersey: Catholic Book Publishing, 2011), 662, note.

14. Anderson, *Out of the Depths*, 83.

The psalmist also confesses his inherent sinfulness: "in guilt I was born, and in sin my mother conceived me" (v. 7). This verse has been interpreted by some, especially the Protestant reformer John Calvin, as teaching the inherent sinfulness of the conjugal act. However, this is not what the psalmist is saying. Rather, it is an example of poetic hyperbole that means "thoroughly sinful,"[15] a confession that "at no time was the psalmist ever without sin."[16] It is an acknowledgment that "everyone is influenced by the brokenness manifest in the family, the nation, the world at large. . . . The condition is inescapably personal and can be cured only when a penitent person casts himself or herself on the mercy of God. . . . Then the forgiving God may perform a new act of creation, giving one a new beginning and putting a new spirit within (cf. Ezek 11:19; 36:28)."[17]

This psalm expresses with depth and beauty the truth of sin as a rejection of God's love. The psalmist offers a poignant example of profound contrition. He recognizes his need for a healing and transformation of heart and spirit that only God can accomplish. It "is surely one of the pearls of the Psalter."[18]

LISTEN TO MY VOICE: JEREMIAH 7:21–26

The prophet Jeremiah, born of a priestly family around the year 650 BC, prophesied during a period of national crisis. He witnessed the reforms of King Josiah (2 Kgs 22–23), only to see the country fall back into idolatry after his death. Led by Nebuchadnezzar, Jerusalem was captured in 598 BC and King Jehoiachin exiled. Against Jeremiah's advice, Zedekiah, the king appointed by the Babylonians, revolted against Babylonian control—Babylon responded by destroying Jerusalem in 587 BC and taking the leading citizens into exile. Jeremiah initially remained in Jerusalem but at some point was exiled to Egypt. We do not know the details of his death. "Arrest, imprisonment, and public disgrace

---

15. Raymond Brown, Joseph Fitzmyer, and Roland Murphy, eds., *New Jerome Biblical Commentary* (Upper Saddle River, NJ: Prentice Hall, 1990), 534.

16. *New American Bible*, 662, note.

17. Anderson, *Out of the Depths*, 84.

18. Anderson, *Out of the Depths*, 81.

were his lot."[19] "Of an affectionate and gentle disposition, . . . this man of peace was for ever at war, with his own people, with kings, priests, false prophets, the nation itself. . . . All this suffering purified his soul of everything unworthy and made it open to God. . . . Jeremiah practiced a really inward and heartfelt religion; this is what makes him near and dear to Christians."[20] The RP includes two passages from Jeremiah, 2:1–13 and the one we will consider now, 7:21–26.

This passage dates from the reign of King Jehoiachin. Here the Lord is rebuking the people for their shallow, external sacrifices: "Heap your burnt offerings upon your sacrifices; eat up the flesh!" (v. 21). He then recalls the Exodus, "In speaking to your fathers on the day I brought them out of the land of Egypt, I gave them no command concerning burnt offering or sacrifice" (v. 22). What was his command at the time of the Exodus? "This rather is what I commanded them: Listen to my voice; then I will be your God and you shall be my people" (v. 23). "Right conduct, rather than formal ritual was God's will concerning his people."[21] However, they did not listen, but "walked in the hardness of their evil hearts and turned their backs, not their faces, to me" (v. 24). The reference here to hardness of heart is characteristic of Jeremiah. "Jeremiah, the prophet most sensitive to the problem of sin, goes so far as to speak of a kind of 'sinful state' of humanity, whereas the other prophets speak only of sinful actions."[22] Although God sent them "untiringly all my servants the prophets," they neither listened nor paid attention. Instead, they "have stiffened their necks and done worse than their fathers" (v. 26). The phrase "stiffened necks" is "synonymous with 'hardness of heart.' External practices and sacrifices have no value unless they are informed by a sincere devotion of the heart." [23]

Here, the sin is essentially a rejection of God's word, a refusal to listen to the Lord. In *The Word of the Lord* (VD, 26), Pope Benedict XVI cited this passage in his discussion of "Sin as a Refusal to Hear the Word of God." This passage is worth quoting in full:

---

19. *New American Bible*, 934.

20. *New Jerusalem Bible*, Henry Wansbrough, ed. (Garden City, NY: Doubleday, 1985), 1171.

21. *New American Bible*, 944 note.

22. Brown et al., *New Jerome Biblical Commentary*, 276.

23. Ibid.

The word of God also inevitably reveals the tragic possibility that human freedom can withdraw from this covenant dialogue with God for which we were created. The divine word also discloses the sin that lurks in the human heart. Quite frequently in both the Old and in the New Testament, we find sin described as a *refusal to hear the word*, as a *breaking of the covenant* and thus as being closed to God who calls us to communion with himself (for example: Dt 28:1–2, 15, 45; 32:1; among the prophets, see: Jer 7:22–28; Ez 2:8; 3:10; 6:3; 13:2; up to the latest: cf. Zech 3:8. For St. Paul, cf. Rom 10:14–18; 1 Thes 2:13). Sacred Scripture shows how man's sin is essentially disobedience and refusal to hear. The radical obedience of Jesus even to his death on the cross (cf. Phil 2:8) completely unmasks this sin. His obedience brings about the New Covenant between God and man, and grants us the possibility of reconciliation. Jesus was sent by the Father as a sacrifice of atonement for our sins and for those of the whole world (cf. 1 Jn 2:2; 4:10; Heb 7:27). We are thus offered the merciful possibility of redemption and the start of a new life in Christ. For this reason it is important that the faithful be taught to acknowledge that the root of sin lies in the refusal to hear the word of the Lord, and to accept in Jesus, the Word of God, the forgiveness which opens us to salvation. (VD, 26)

Jeremiah witnessed in his people this refusal, this breaking, this rejection of communion with God. He knew from his own experience God's mercy and the possibility of a transformed life, foreshadowing the definitive mercy and new life experienced in Christ.

A NEW HEART AND A NEW SPIRIT: EZEKIEL, 36:23–28

Ezekiel, Jeremiah's younger contemporary, was among those taken into exile to Babylon, where he "became the first prophet to be commissioned outside Judah or Israel."[24] His early prophecies contended that the destruction of Jerusalem and the Temple and the exile to Babylon were punishment for the nation's sin and idolatry. In his later prophecies he "argues that the Judahites who embrace his preaching are the people whom the Lord has chosen as a new Israel, enlivened by a new heart, imbued with new breath (chaps. 36–37), and restored to a re-created land, Temple, and covenant relationship (chaps. 40–48)."[25] The RP includes

---

24. *New American Bible*, 1013.
25. Ibid.

several passages from Ezekiel, 11:14–21, 18:20–32, and the passage we will look at, 36:23–28.

This passage begins with the assertion that God will vindicate his name—his glory and honor—among the nations who saw Judah's defeat as a sign of God's weakness. "I will prove the holiness of my great name," says the Lord, "profaned among the nations, in whose midst you have profaned it"; then they "shall know that I am the LORD, says the Lord GOD" (v. 23). He then promises to restore them to their own land. He will cleanse his people from their impurities and from their idols, giving them "a new heart," "natural hearts" in place of their "stony hearts," and " a new spirit" (v. 26). The promise of a new heart and a new spirit point to a complete transformation: "The heart is the seat of thinking and loving, so it will be a way of looking at life from God's point of view. The new spirit is the power to live as an entire nation, not just as individuals."[26] God is creating nothing less than a new people, a people "no longer disposed to repeating Israel's wicked past (chap. 20). To make this restoration permanent, God replaces Israel's rebellious and obdurate interiority ('heart of stone') with an interiority ('heart of flesh') susceptible to and animated by God's intention ('my spirit,' v. 27)."[27]

The references to this passage in the *Catechism* highlight its importance in preparing for the person and work of Christ. This prophecy by Ezekiel is one of the prophetic proclamations of "a radical redemption of the People of God, purification from all their infidelities, a salvation which will include all the nations" (CCC, 64). It acknowledges the reality of the human heart which "is heavy and hardened. God must give man a new heart (Ezek 36:26–27). Conversion is first of all a work of the grace of God who makes our hearts return to him: 'Restore us to thyself, O LORD, that we may be restored!' (Lam 5:21)" (CCC, 1432). Finally, the promise of a new spirit anticipates the gift of the Holy Spirit. "The prophetic texts that directly concern the sending of the Holy Spirit are oracles by which God speaks to the heart of his people in the language of the promise, with the accents of 'love and fidelity' (cf. Ezek 11:19; 36:25–28; 37:1–14; Jer 31:31–34; and cf. Joel 3:1–5)" (CCC, 715). The fullness of the Spirit which Jesus received "was not to

---

26. Brown et al., *New Jerome Biblical Commentary*, 325.

27. *New American Bible*, 1051.

remain uniquely the Messiah's, but was to be communicated to the whole messianic people (Ezek 36:25–27; Joel 3:1–2)" (CCC, 1287).

Ezekiel's prophecy highlights important aspects of the Sacrament of Penance: he acknowledges the painful consequences and punishment consequent upon sin, but he also looks ahead to the healing and transformation accomplished through the power of God communicated in the celebration of the sacrament.

A GOD OF PARDONS: NEHEMIAH 9:1–20

Nehemiah was one of the leaders of Israel following its return from exile in Babylon. Nehemiah and Ezra together "helped make it possible for Judaism to maintain its identity during the difficult days of the Restoration. Ezra was the great religious reformer who succeeded in establishing the Torah as the constitution of the returned community. Nehemiah, governor of the province of Judah, was the man of action who rebuilt the walls of Jerusalem and introduced necessary administrative reforms."[28] Nehemiah's first term as governor was from 445 to 432 BC, but his second term was of unknown length. The communal penitential service celebrated by the returnees is the final Old Testament passage we will consider.

The preparation for the penitential service is the reading of the law described in Nehemiah 8. "Ezra read clearly from the book of the law of God, interpreting it so that all could understand what was read" (Neh 8:8). This reading included the command to celebrate the Feast of Booths, "so the entire assembly of the returned exiles made booths and dwelt in them" (Neh 8:17). The penitential liturgy follows this celebration. "The children of Israel gathered together fasting and in sackcloth, their heads covered with dust" (9:1). Those who had contracted marriages with foreigners "separated themselves from all who were of foreign extraction, then stood forward and confessed their sin and the guilt deeds of their fathers" (9:2). Once they were all assembled, the book of the law was read for a fourth of the day, and "during another fourth part they made their confession and prostrated themselves before the LORD their God" (9:3).

---

28. Ibid., 479.

The Levites exhort the people to bless the Lord, and they answer, "Blessed is your glorious name, and exalted above all blessing and praise" (v. 5). Ezra the priest then offers a long prayer recounting God's faithfulness to Israel, beginning with creation, the covenant with Abraham, the deliverance from Egypt, the giving of "just ordinances, firm laws, good statutes and commandments . . . by the hand of Moses your servant" (9:13–14). The historical summary concludes with the manna from heaven, "water from the rock," and entrance into the Promised Land, "which you had sworn with upraised hand to give them" (9:15). Ezra then recounts their sin. "But they, our fathers, proved to be insolent. . . . They refused to obey and no longer remembered the miracles you had worked for them. They stiffened their necks and turned their heads to return to their slavery in Egypt" (9:16–17). Despite these sins and the worship of a molten calf (9:18), God did not forsake them (9:17, 19), for he is "a God of pardons, gracious and compassionate, slow to anger and rich in mercy" (9:17). God continued to bless them, bestowing on them his good spirit "to give them understanding," feeding them with manna and quenching their thirst (9:20). God's continued blessing in the face of insolence and disobedience reveals the compassionate mercy of God praised in a hymn of the early church: "If we are unfaithful, he remains faithful, for he cannot deny himself" (2 Tim 2:13).

This Old Testament penitential service reveals many important aspects of the Sacrament of Penance: the power of God's word, true contrition, and the importance of a grateful remembrance of God's past goodness. It also presents a God who is compassionate, rich in mercy, patient and forgiving—in the words of the present formula of absolution, "the Father of mercies." It also anticipates the structure of the Rite for Reconciliation of Several Penitents with Individual Confession and Absolution: Introductory Rites including a Greeting and response (9:5), the Celebration of the Word of God (9:3, 6–20), a General Confession of Sins (9:2–3), and a Proclamation of Praise for God's Mercy (9:19–20). Old Testament penitential liturgies such as Nehemiah 9 reveal the communal dimension of penance, as Pope Bl. Paul VI noted: "The social aspect of penitence is not lacking in the Old Testament. In fact, the penitential liturgies of the Old Covenant are not only a collective awareness of sin but constitute in reality a condition for belonging to the people of God."[29]

CONCLUSION

The Old Testament passages that we have considered in this chapter anticipate and reveal many aspects of the Sacrament of Penance. We see the three acts of the penitent, the contrition of kings (David), priests (Ezra), prophets (Jeremiah and Ezekiel), and the whole people of God (Nehemiah). We hear the private (David) and public (Nehemiah) confession of sins. We witness acts of satisfaction as sinners resume the journey toward holiness with the Lord. We hear proclaimed the compassionate and forgiving nature of our Lord. And with the children of Israel we say, "Blessed is your glorious name, and exalted above all blessing and praise" (Neh 9:5).

Activity

Review the different names of this sacrament and the different Old Testament readings we have looked at. If you were doing a presentation on this sacrament based on the different names, which readings or verses would you choose to illustrate each of the names?

1. Conversion _____

2. Confession _____

3. Forgiveness_____

4. Reconciliation _____

5. Penance_____

---

29. Paul VI, Apostolic Constitution *Paenitemini* on Fast and Abstinence, chapter 1.

Chapter 5

Penance and Reconciliation: Signs and Symbols

"The Sacrament of Penance is an eloquent sign of our desire for perfection, contemplation, fraternal communion and apostolic mission" (PMDM, 10). It is comprised of signs through which the Holy Spirit "puts both the faithful and the ministers into a living relationship with Christ, the Word and Image of the Father, so that they can live out the meaning of what they hear, contemplate, and do in celebration" (CCC, 1101). The sacrament includes many different kinds of signs. The participants—the penitent, the priest, and the people of God—are central signs of the sacrament. Gestures—the sign of the cross and the imposition of hands—are another type of sign. The spoken word is a third type of sign, including the penitent's examination of conscience, confession, and act of contrition and the formula of absolution spoken by the priest. The satisfaction (or "penance") assigned by the priest is a fourth kind of sign. On a larger scale, even the two forms of the sacrament—reconciliation of individual penitents and reconciliation of several penitents with individual confession and absolution—are sacramental signs. Recognizing and understanding this diversity of signs will enable us to "pass from its signs to the mystery they contain (MND, 17)," to enter more deeply into the mystery of God's mercy and forgiveness, and to experience the conversion and transformation our hearts desire. We will begin our discussion of the sacramental signs with the participants: the priest, the penitent, and the people of God.

THE PARTICIPANTS: THE PRIEST

The priest is "an 'icon' of Christ the priest" (CCC, 1142) through whom "the presence of Christ as head of the Church is made visible in the midst of the community of believers" (CCC, 1549). In the Sacrament of Penance, the priest "is the sign and the instrument of God's merciful love for the sinner" (CCC, 1465). St. John Paul II describes him as both "judge and healer, a figure of God the Father welcoming and forgiving the one who returns" (RaP, 31.III). In the Sacrament of Penance he is an icon of several biblical images: "When he celebrates the sacrament of Penance, the priest is fulfilling the ministry of the Good Shepherd who seeks the lost sheep, of the Good Samaritan who binds up wounds, of the Father who awaits the prodigal son and welcomes him on his return, and of the just and impartial judge whose judgment is both just and merciful" (CCC, 1465).

In *The Face of Mercy* (*Misericordiae Vultus*), Pope Francis develops the image of the priest as the father of the prodigal son. "Every confessor must accept the faithful as the father in the parable of the prodigal son: a father who runs out to meet his son despite the fact that he has squandered away his inheritance. Confessors are called to embrace the repentant son who comes back home and to express the joy of having him back again. Let us never tire of also going out to the other son who stands outside, incapable of rejoicing, in order to explain to him that his judgment is severe and unjust and meaningless in light of the father's boundless mercy. . . . In short, confessors are called to be a sign of the primacy of mercy always, everywhere, and in every situation, no matter what."[1]

St. John Paul II also emphasizes the sign value of the priest, citing an abundance of biblical images. "The Christ whom he makes present and who accomplishes the mystery of the forgiveness of sins is the Christ who appears as the brother of man (cf. Mt 12:49f.; Mk 3:33f.; Lk 8:20f.; Rom 8:29: 'the firstborn among many brethren'), the merciful high priest, faithful and compassionate (cf. Heb 2:17; 4:15), the shepherd intent on finding the lost sheep (cf. Mt 18:12f.; Lk 15:4–6), the physician who heals and comforts (cf. Lk 5:31f.), the one master who teaches the truth and reveals the ways of God (cf. Mt 22:16), the judge of the living and the dead (Acts 10:42), who judges according to the truth and not according to appearances (cf. Jn 8:16)" (RaP, 29). These biblical images reveal the complexity of the priest's ministry. In imitation of Christ he responds to the state and circumstances of each penitent, when necessary helping him "to make a complete confession," encouraging him to have sincere sorrow for his sins, offering appropriate counsel to help the penitent begin "a new life, and, where necessary, giv[e] instruction

---

1. Francis, *Misericordiae Vultus*, Bull of Indiction of the Jubilee of Mercy (no. 17), accessed April 14, 2015, http://www.iubilaeummisericordiae.va/content/gdm/en/bolla.html.

on the duties of the Christian life" (RP, 18). Finally, he leads the penitent to "make due restitution" if he has brought harm or scandal to others (RP, 18).

To be this "living sign of Christ the servant"[2] imposes a serious responsibility on the priest. He begins by uniting himself "to the intention and charity of Christ" (CCC, 1466; PO, 13). To this he should add "a proven knowledge of Christian behavior, experience of human affairs, respect and sensitivity toward the one who has fallen; he must love the truth, be faithful to the Magisterium of the Church, and lead the penitent with patience toward healing and full maturity. He must pray and do penance for his penitent, entrusting him to the Lord's mercy" (CCC, 1466). Finally, like Christ, he "must encourage the faithful to come to the sacrament of Penance" and at same time "must make [himself] available to celebrate this sacrament each time Christians reasonably ask for it" (CCC, 1464).

An effective confessor takes on the heart of the Good Shepherd who calls each of his sheep by name, an acknowledgement of each Christian's unique path of discipleship. In *The Joy of the Gospel*, Pope Francis reminded "priests that the confessional must not be a torture chamber but rather an encounter with the Lord's mercy which spurs us on to do our best. A small step, in the midst of great human limitations, can be more pleasing to God than a life which appears outwardly in order but moves through the day without confronting great difficulties. Everyone needs to be touched by the comfort and attraction of God's saving love, which is mysteriously at work in each person, above and beyond their faults and failings" (EG, 44). St. John Paul II summed up the challenge and blessing of this ministry: "This is undoubtedly the most difficult and sensitive, the most exhausting and demanding ministry of the priest, but also one of the most beautiful and consoling" (RaP, 29).

THE PARTICIPANTS: THE PENITENT

Just as the priest is the sign of the mercy of God the Father and of Christ, our merciful high priest, so the penitent is a sign of the sinner seeking mercy. He is, writes St. John Paul II, "a sign of the person's

---

2. Jean Corbon, *The Wellspring of Worship*, trans. Matthew J. O'Connell (San Francisco: Ignatius Press, 1988), 169.

revealing of self as a sinner in the sight of God and the church, of facing his own sinful condition in the eyes of God" (RaP, 31.III). As such, he is a sign of the truthfulness and humility of man before God, as St. Bernard of Clairvaux wrote: "No one is saved without self-knowledge, since it is the source of that humility on which salvation depends, and of the fear of the Lord that is as much the beginning of salvation as of wisdom. . . . For you cannot love what you do not know, nor possess what you do not love. Know yourself and you will have a wholesome fear of God; know him and you will also love him."[3]

The penitent, like the priest, is a sign of such biblical images as the prodigal son and the repentant thief, images that we find in one of the options for the act of contrition: "Father of mercy, like the prodigal son I return to you and say: 'I have sinned against you and am no longer worthy to be called your son.' Christ Jesus, Savior of the world, I pray with the repentant thief to whom you promised Paradise: 'Lord, remember me in your kingdom.' Holy Spirit, fountain of love, I call on you with trust: 'Purify my heart, and help me to walk as a child of light'" (RP, 88). In this prayer the penitent speaks the words of the humbled prodigal son returning to his father (Lk 15:19) and the words of the thief crucified with Christ who acknowledges Jesus' innocence and the justice of his own punishment (Lk 23:40–41). The prayer also reveals forgiveness as a Trinitarian mystery, addressing first the "Father of mercy," then "Christ Jesus, Savior of the world," and finally the "Holy Spirit, fountain of love." The penitent is a sign of humility rooted in the truth and of confidence in the infinite mercy of God.

THE PARTICIPANTS: THE PEOPLE OF GOD

The Church by its very nature is penitential. The Church, "having sinners in its midst, is at the same time holy and in need of cleansing, and so is unceasingly intent on repentance and reform" (RP, 3). Her constant pursuit of repentance and renewal is accomplished and perfected "in many different ways" (RP, 4). It "share[s] in the sufferings of Christ by enduring [its] own difficulties, carr[ies] out works of mercy and charity, and adopt[s] ever more fully the outlook of the Gospel message" (RP, 4). The *Catechism* elaborates on the different ways that the Church

---

3. Bernard of Clairvaux, *On the Song of Songs II: Sermons 21–46*, trans. Kilian Walsh, OCSO (Kalamazoo, MI: Cistercian Publications, 1983), 181.

expresses her penitential identity. She follows the teaching of Scripture and the Fathers in practicing prayer, fasting, and almsgiving, "which express conversion in relation to oneself, to God, and to others" (CCC, 1434). Other daily efforts at conversion include "gestures of reconciliation, concern for the poor, the exercise and defense of justice and right, by the admission of faults to one's brethren, fraternal correction, revision of life, examination of conscience, spiritual direction, acceptance of suffering, endurance of persecution for the sake of righteousness" (CCC, 1435). Finally, any simple yet sincere act of worship and devotion such as praying the Our Father or reading Scripture "revives the spirit of conversion and repentance within us and contributes to the forgiveness of our sins" (CCC, 1437). "Thus the people of God become in the world a sign of conversion to God" (RP, 4).

The Church is God's instrument for gathering and reconciling "his children scattered throughout the world" (Eucharistic Prayer III). But, as St. John Paul II has noted, "the church, if she is to be reconciling, must begin by being a reconciled church. Beneath this simple and indicative expression lies the conviction that the church, in order ever more effectively to proclaim and propose reconciliation to the world, must become ever more genuinely a community of disciples of Christ (even though it were only 'the little flock' of the first days), united in the commitment to be continually converted to the Lord and to live as new people in the spirit and practice of reconciliation" (RaP, 9). All of these diverse forms of penance, public and private, individual and communal, formal and spontaneous, are celebrated "in [the] liturgy when the faithful confess that they are sinners and ask pardon of God and of their brothers and sisters. This happens in penitential services, in the proclamation of the word of God, in prayer, and in the penitential aspects of the Eucharistic celebration" (RP, 4), such as the Penitential Rite (e.g., "I confess to almighty God . . . ") and the prayer said quietly by the priest as he washes his hands, "Wash me, O Lord, from my iniquity and cleanse me from my sin" (RM, Order of Mass, 4 and 28). In these ways the Church perfects herself in holiness and humility and calls the world to be reconciled with its Creator.

ACTS OF THE PENITENT

Essential to the Sacrament of Penance are the three acts of the penitent—contrition, confession, and satisfaction. "Penance requires . . . the sinner to endure all things willingly, be contrite of heart, confess with the lips, and practice complete humility and fruitful satisfaction" (CCC, 1450). Each of these acts constitutes a distinctive sign of the sacrament.

Contrition

The RP defines contrition as "heartfelt sorrow and aversion for the sin committed along with the intention of sinning no more" (RP, 6a). Contrition initiates "a profound change of the whole person by which one begins to consider, judge, and arrange his life according to the holiness and love of God, made manifest in his Son in the last days and given to us in abundance (see Heb 1:2; Col 1:19 and passim)" (RP, 6a). Among the acts of the penitent it is paramount (CCC, 1451), for "the genuineness of penance depends on this heartfelt contrition. For conversion should affect a person from within so that it may progressively enlighten him and render him continually more like Christ" (RP, 6a). This decisive return to God "has in the sacrament of penance its visible sign" (RaP, 31.III). It is born in the depths of one's conscience, and so to better understand contrition we must examine the Church's understanding of conscience.

Conscience is "man's sanctuary" (VS, 54), a law written on his heart by God: "To obey it is the very dignity of man; according to it he will be judged (cf. Rom 2:14–16)" (VS, 54). It constitutes an "interior *dialog of man with himself*" (VS, 58, italics original), and "only the person himself knows what his own response is to the voice of conscience" (VS, 57). At the same time, "it is also a *dialog of man with God*" (VS, 58, italics original). St. Bonaventure said that "conscience is like God's herald and messenger; it does not command things on its own authority, but commands them as coming from God's authority, like a herald when he proclaims the edict of the king. This is why conscience has binding force" (VS, 58). Sin turns man in on himself and away from God, but conscience "opens him to the call, to the voice of God. In this, and not in anything else, lies the entire mystery and the dignity of the moral conscience; in being the place, the sacred place where God speaks to man" (VS, 58).

This means that "the rectitude and clarity of the penitent's conscience" is "an indispensable condition" for heartfelt repentance (RaP, 31.III). "True and genuine repentance" requires a realization that sin contradicts the law of God written on one's heart, an acceptance of "a personal and responsible experience of this contrast," an admission "not only that 'sin exists' but also 'I have sinned,'" an acknowledgement of a division in one's conscience that touches one's entire being, separating the sinner from God and one's brothers and sisters (RaP, 31.III). The fruit of this profoundly interior dialog with oneself and with God has its own sacramental sign, "the act traditionally called the examination of conscience, an act that must never be one of anxious psychological introspection, but a sincere and calm comparison with the interior moral law, with the evangelical norms proposed by the church, with Jesus Christ himself, who is our teacher and model of life, and with the heavenly Father, who calls us to goodness and perfection" (RaP, 31.III). In practical terms, such an examination is best made "in the light of the Word of God" (CCC, 1454). The *Catechism* recommends the following passages: Matthew 5–7; Romans 12–15; 1 Corinthians 12–13; Galatians 5, and Ephesians 4–6 (CCC, 1454, 53n). The RP also includes an examination of conscience divided into three sections, each based on a word of the Lord: First, "You shall love the Lord your God with your whole heart"; second, "Love one another as I have loved you"; and third, "Be perfect as your Father is perfect" (RP, Appendix III).

Contrition, then, is the fruit of a well-formed and humble conscience, and it is "the most important act of the penitent" (RP, 6a). Depending on its inner dynamic, contrition is either "perfect" or "imperfect." Both are the "gift of God, a prompting of the Holy Spirit" (CCC, 1453). Perfect contrition, also known as contrition of charity, "arises from a love by which God is loved above all else" (CCC, 1452). Imperfect contrition, also known as attrition, "is born of the consideration of sin's ugliness or the fear of eternal damnation and the other penalties threatening the sinner (contrition of fear)" (CCC, 1453).

The external sign of contrition is the prayer of the penitent (this is often referred to as the "act of contrition"; the rite does not use this term), an expression of the penitent's sorrow. The RP gives ten options, although the penitent may use one of "these or similar words" (RP, 45). The first is perhaps the most familiar: "My God, I am sorry for my sins with all my heart" (RP, 45.1). Another option is from Psalm 25: "Remember that your compassion, O Lord, and your love are from of old. In your kindness remember me, because of your goodness, O Lord" (Ps 25:6-7). The second line can also be translated "According to your mercy remember me, for your goodness' sake, O Lord" (RSV, 2nd Catholic ed.). The Hebrew word that is translated "kindness" or "mercy" is *hesed*. Whenever it is used of the Lord in the Old Testament, it is always "in connection with the covenant that God established with Israel (DiM, n. 52)" and so had a certain legal connotation. But if Israel broke the covenant, God's juridical commitment ceased. "But precisely at this point, *hesed* in ceasing to be a juridical obligation, revealed its deeper aspect: it showed itself as what it was in the beginning, that is, as love that gives, love more powerful than betrayal, grace stronger than sin" (DiM, n. 52). "The Old Testament encourages people suffering from misfortune, especially those weighed down by sin—as also the whole of Israel, which had entered into the covenant with God—to appeal for mercy, and enables them to count upon it: it reminds them of His mercy in times of failure and loss of trust" (DiM, 4).

The Church Fathers have given us beautiful commentaries on Psalm 25's appeal to God's mercy. Theodoret of Cyr paraphrases these verses thus: "According to your great mercy, remember me; remember not my sin but me in loving fashion."[4] St. Augustine offers a more expansive paraphrase: "Please do remember me, not in the anger of which I am worthy, but in your mercy, which is worthy of you, and this 'because of your goodness, O Lord,' not because of what is due to me, Lord, but because of your own goodness."[5] "In these words a noble and orthodox sentiment seems to shine forth on us," writes Cassiodorus, "for no one attains God's grace by his own merits. By speaking of God's 'mercy, which is at the beginning of the world,' the church continually praises the Lord as the donor of mercies who does not as a prior step take up people's deserving deeds but grants first his own gifts."[6]

---

4. Craig A. Blaising and Carmen S. Hardin, *Psalms 1–50*, Old Testament VII, Ancient Christian Commentary on Scripture (Downers Grove, IL: InterVarsity Press, 2008), 195.

5. Ibid.

6. Ibid., 194–195.

Digging into the Catechism

Read the section on moral conscience, CCC 1776–1802.

1. How does the Catechism define conscience (1778)?

2. What are the three aspects of conscience (1780)?

3. What three sources help us form our conscience (1785)?

4. What three rules always apply when choosing in accord with conscience (1789)?

5. What are some of the sources of errors in judgment (1792)?

Confession of Sins

The second act of the penitent is the confession of sins, an act "which comes from true knowledge of self before God and from contrition for those sins. . . . [This] inner examination of heart and the outward accusation must be made in the light of God's mercy" (RP, 6b). The penitent is required to confess all grave (mortal) sins, "even if they are most secret and have been committed against the last two precepts of the Decalogue; for these sins sometimes wound the soul more grievously and are more dangerous than those which are committed openly" (CCC, 1456). When penitents intend to confess all known sins, even if they forget some, "they undoubtedly place all of them before the divine mercy for pardon" (CCC, 1456), but if they intentionally withhold some, they place nothing before the throne of mercy, "for if the sick person is too ashamed to show his wound to the doctor," wrote St. Jerome, "the medicine cannot heal what it does not know" (CCC, 1456).

This confession of the penitent "has the value of a sign: a sign of the meeting of the sinner with the mediation of the church in the person of the minister, a sign of the person's revealing of self as a sinner in the sight of God and the church, of facing his own sinful condition in the eyes of God" (RaP, 31.III). The confession of sins manifests a "legitimate and natural need, inherent in the human heart, to open oneself to another" (RaP, 31.III). But it is much more than that. "It is a liturgical act, solemn in its dramatic nature, yet humble and sober in the grandeur of its meaning. It is the act of the prodigal son who returns to his Father and is welcomed by him with the kiss of peace. It is an act of honesty and courage. It is an act of entrusting oneself, beyond sin, to the mercy that forgives" (RaP, 31.III).

This humble, honest, and courageous act makes one a coworker with God, the Father of mercies. This is how St. Augustine described becoming a coworker with God:

> Whoever confesses his sins . . . is already working with God. God indicts your sins; if you also indict them, you are joined with God. Man and sinner are, so to speak, two realities: when you hear "man"—this is what God has made; when you hear "sinner"—this is what man himself has made. Destroy what you have made, so that God may save what he has made. . . . When you begin to abhor what you have made, it is then that your good works are beginning, since you are accusing yourself of your evil works. The beginning of good works is the confession of evil works. You do the truth and come to the light. (Augustine, *In evangelium Johannis tractatus*, in JP Migne, Patrologia Latina [Paris: 1841–1855], 35, 1491; cited in CCC, 1458)

Every penitent that comes to the light shines with the light of Christ and radiates his light to the world.

Act of Penance—Satisfaction

The third act of the penitent is the act of penance, also known as satisfaction or simply penance. It is an acknowledgement that the effects of sin are manifold, hurting the sinner himself, damaging his relationship with God and neighbor, and often wronging his neighbor. Absolution removes sin, but it does not repair all of the damage wrought by sin. The penitent completes "true conversion" through "expiation for the sins committed, by amendment of life, and also by rectifying injuries done" (RP, 6c). Expiation or satisfaction is a matter of both justice and healing. Justice may require the penitent to "return stolen goods, restore the reputation of someone slandered, [or] pay compensation for injuries" (CCC, 1459). But it is also medicinal, for "it is necessary that the act of penance really be a remedy for sin and a help to renewal of life" (RP, 6c). Both aspects—justice and healing—require that "the kind and extent of the expiation must be suited to the personal condition of penitents so that they may restore the order that they have upset and through the corresponding remedy be cured of the sickness from which they suffered" (RP, 6c).

In determining the act of penance, the priest must take into account several different factors: the personal situation of the penitent, his spiritual good, and the nature and seriousness of the sins committed (CCC, 1460). The act of penance may include "prayer, an offering, works of mercy, service of neighbor, voluntary self-denial, sacrifices, and above all the patient acceptance of the cross we must bear" (CCC, 1460). Penances that involve love of neighbor "underline the fact that sin and its forgiveness have a social aspect" (RP, 18). Whatever the penance, it is never solely the work of man, as the Council of Trent affirmed:

> The satisfaction that we make for our sins, however, is not so much ours as though it were not done through Jesus Christ. We who can do nothing ourselves, as if just by ourselves, can do all things with the cooperation of "him who strengthens" us. Thus man has nothing of which to boast, but all our boasting is in Christ . . . in whom we make satisfaction by bringing forth "fruits that befit repentance." These fruits have their efficacy from him, by him they are offered to the Father, and through him they are accepted by the Father. (CCC, 1460)

Ultimately, the satisfaction "should serve not only as atonement for past sins but also as an aid to a new life and an antidote for weakness" (RP, 18). In this way the penitent incarnates the words of the Apostle Paul: "'forgetting the things that are behind' (Phil 3:13), [he] again become[s] part of the mystery of salvation and press[es] on toward the things that are to come" (RP, 6c).

St. John Paul II explains the different meanings of this liturgical sign. Addressing the minister of the sacrament, he insists that acts of satisfaction should on the one hand remain "simple and humble" while on the other hand expressing "more clearly all that they signify" (RaP, 31.III). First of all, it is "the sign of the personal commitment that the Christian has made to God in the sacrament to begin a new life" (RaP, 31.III). For this reason "acts of penance should not be reduced to mere formulas to be recited, but should consist of acts of worship, charity, mercy or reparation" (RaP, 31.III). Second, penance is a sign of the pardoned sinner's ability "to join his own physical and spiritual mortification—which has been sought after or at least accepted—to the passion of Jesus, who has obtained the forgiveness for him" (RaP, 31.III). Finally, it is a sign of the ongoing character of conversion, a reminder "that even after absolution there remains in the Christian a dark area due to the wound of sin, to the imperfection of love in repentance, to the weakening of the spiritual faculties. It is an area in which there still operates an infectious source of sin which must always be fought with mortification and penance" (RaP, 31.III). "This," he concludes, "is the meaning of the humble but sincere act of satisfaction" (RaP, 31.III).

Signs of Satisfaction

List the three meanings or "signs" of penance/satisfaction.

1. _____

2. _____

3. _____

What are some examples of a penance/satisfaction for the sin of judging others that would satisfy these three meanings?

Absolution

The forgiveness of sin is accomplished by the action of God through the Church. Absolution consists of three sacramental signs: the words of absolution, the imposition of hands, and the sign of the cross. We will begin with the formula of absolution:

> God, the Father of mercies,
> through the death and the resurrection of his Son
> has reconciled the world to himself
> and sent the Holy Spirit among us
> for the forgiveness of sins;
> through the ministry of the Church
> may God give you pardon and peace,
> and I absolve you from your sins
> in the name of the Father, and of the Son, +
> and of the Holy Spirit. (RP, 46)

These words express the essential aspects of this sacrament: "the Father of mercies is the source of all forgiveness. He effects the reconciliation of sinners through the Passover of his Son and the gift of his Spirit, through the prayer and ministry of the Church" (CCC, 1449). Once again the Church confesses the presence and work of the Trinity in sacramental celebrations. We can say that it is the triune God's generous answer to the prayer of the contrite sinner: "Lord Jesus Christ, you are the Lamb of God; you take away the sins for the world. Through the grace of the Holy Spirit restore me to friendship with your Father, cleanse me from every stain of sin in the blood you shed for me, and raise me to new life for the glory of your name" (RP, 91).

The formula of absolution is drawn from several New Testament passages. The description of God as the Father of mercies comes from 2 Corinthians 1:3: "Blessed be the God and Father of our Lord Jesus Christ, the Father of mercies and God of all comfort" (RSV, 2nd Catholic ed.). The anamnesis, "through the death and resurrection of his Son has reconciled the world to himself" recalls 2 Corinthians 5:19: "God was reconciling the world to himself in Christ." The sending of the Spirit for the forgiveness of sins is a reference to Jesus' appearance to the disciples gathered behind locked doors "for fear of the Jews" (Jn 20.19). Jesus "breathed on them and said to them, 'Receive the holy Spirit. Whose sins you forgive are forgiven them, and whose sins you retain are retained'" (Jn 20:22–23). The scriptural basis for the formula of absolution is a powerful illustration of one of the guiding principles of the Second Vatican Council in its reform of the liturgy, the importance of Sacred Scripture, for as the Council noted, "the prayers, collects, and liturgical songs are scriptural in their inspiration and their force" (SC, 24). The reference to "their force" is a further reminder of Christ's presence in the Scriptures. The priest, acting in the person of Christ the head, speaks the words of the Word that proclaim and bring about both pardon and peace. The Rite summarizes the rich language of sign contained in the formula of absolution: "The form of absolution *indicates* that the reconciliation of the penitent comes from the mercy of the Father; it *shows* the connection between the reconciliation of the sinner and the paschal mystery of Christ; it *stresses* the role of the Holy Spirit in the forgiveness of sins; finally, it *underlines* the ecclesial aspect of the sacrament because reconciliation with God is asked for and given through the ministry of the Church" (RP, 19; italics added).

The formula of absolution is accompanied by two gestures. The first is the gesture of the epiclesis:[7] "the priest extends his hands over the penitent's head (or at least extends his right hand)" (RP, 46). The New Testament reveals the rich variety of meanings of this sacramental

---

7. The epiclesis and its accompanying gesture are discussed in detail in chapter 2.

sign. Jesus healed the sick and blessed children by laying hands on them (Mk 6:5; 8:23, 10:16), and he empowered the Apostles to do the same (Mk 16:18; Acts 5:12; 14:3). In the Acts of the Apostles, the Holy Spirit is imparted through the imposition of hands (Acts 8:17–19; 13:3; 19:6; cf. 1 Tim and 2 Tim). The Letter to the Hebrews describes the laying on of hands as one of the basic teachings about Christ (6:2). "The Church has kept this sign of the all-powerful outpouring of the Holy Spirit in its sacramental epicleses" (CCC, 699). The epicletic words and gesture are part of every sacrament.

The outpouring of the Holy Spirit in the Sacrament of Penance, as in all of the sacraments, flows from the Paschal Mystery: "The wound suffered by sinners, along with the wounds in their brothers, has been endured by Jesus in his death, and it is from this crucified love that the Spirit who gives communion streams forth."[8] Furthermore, this epicletic moment is a personal encounter with divine love, for the Holy Spirit "is in his person 'the forgiveness of our sins': where the relationship with the Father has been lacking or has even been broken, the Spirit, who is 'the Father's tender love,' pours himself out and becomes the living bond of love that unites persons. He is the blood of communion that causes the members of the body to draw life from the life of the Father."[9] It is the Spirit who brings about our reconciliation with God and with the Church. "The epiclesis proper to this sacrament—and how inattentive we are to it!—consists in this outpouring of the Holy Spirit. . . . In the key moment of the 'absolution' everything is 'loosed' because everything is set free by the communion that is the Spirit of the Lord. The priest's prayer is a true epicletic prayer."[10]

The final sacramental sign of absolution is the sign of the cross,[11] traced over the penitent as the priest concludes the formula of absolution "in the name of the Father, and of the Son, + and of the Holy Spirit" (RP, 46). This element of absolution seems to have appeared in the thirteenth century.[12] St. Thomas Aquinas recommended it "as a fitting accompaniment to absolution," explaining "that such an action would

---

8. Corbon, *The Wellspring of Worship*, 169.

9. Ibid.

10. Ibid.

11. For an introduction to the sign of the cross, see the corresponding section in chapter 2.

12. Monti, *A Sense of the Sacred*, 153.

signify that 'sins are forgiven through the blood of Christ crucified.'"[13] He also suggested adding the accompanying words, "in the name of the Father, and of the Son, and of the Holy Spirit" to the absolution formula, elements that became part of the official rite in 1614.

The Holy Spirit acts through these sacramental signs to bring the penitent "into a living relationship with Christ, the Word and Image of the Father" (CCC, 1101), effecting a saving encounter with the Trinity. "The sacramental formula 'I absolve you' and the imposition of the hand and the Sign of the Cross made over the penitent show that at this moment the contrite and converted sinner comes into contact with the power and mercy of God. It is the moment at which, in response to the penitent, the Trinity becomes present in order to blot out sin and restore innocence. And the saving power of the passion, death and resurrection of Jesus is also imparted to the penitent as the 'mercy stronger than sin and offense'" (RaP, 31.III). In this one moment the entirety of the Christian mystery, the mystery of the Trinity and the Paschal Mystery, becomes present for the sake of one "for whom Christ died" (Rom 14:15).

The words and gestures of the priest constitute a twofold sign: first, an efficacious sign "of the intervention of the Father in every absolution"; and second, "the sign of the 'resurrection' from 'spiritual death' which is renewed each time that the sacrament of penance is administered" (RaP, 31.III). Faith and faith alone assures us that at the moment of absolution "every sin is forgiven and blotted out by the mysterious intervention of the Savior" (RaP, 31.III). This assurance of forgiveness is guaranteed by the character of God. "Mercy in itself, as a perfection of the infinite God, is also infinite. Also infinite therefore and inexhaustible is the Father's readiness to receive the prodigal children who return to His home. Infinite are the readiness and power of forgiveness which flow continually from the marvelous value of the sacrifice of the Son. No human sin can prevail over this power or even limit it. On the part of man only a lack of good will can limit it, a lack of readiness to be converted and to repent, in other words persistence in obstinacy, opposing grace and truth, especially in the face of the witness of the cross and resurrection of Christ" (DV, 13). The infinite mercy of God never ceases to amaze and humble us.

---

13. Ibid.

Forms of Celebration of the Sacrament

As we noted in chapter 4, the RP provides two rites or forms for reconciliation. The first form is the rite for reconciling individual penitents, and the second form is the rite for reconciling several penitents with individual confession and absolution. Each option constitutes a sign of distinct aspects of the sacrament.

The first form more clearly signifies the sacrament as a "personal decision and commitment" (RaP, 32). The different elements of the sacrament such as the dialogue between the priest and penitent, the choice of biblical texts, and the forms of satisfaction can be chosen to "make the sacramental celebration correspond more closely to the concrete situation of the penitent" (RaP, 32). This in turn means that the celebration can correspond to "the different reasons that bring a Christian to sacramental penance: a need for personal reconciliation and readmission to friendship with God by regaining the grace lost by sin; a need to check one's spiritual progress and sometimes a need for a more accurate discernment of one's vocation; on many other occasions a need and a desire to escape from a state of spiritual apathy and religious crisis" (RaP, 32). St. John Paul II suggests that this form also makes "it possible to link the sacrament of penance with something which is different but readily linked with it: I am referring to spiritual direction" (RaP, 32). In these various ways this form is a sign of each individual's unique path of holiness.

The rite for reconciling several penitents with individual confession and absolution is a sign of other aspects of the sacrament. This form offers a fuller liturgy of the word: two readings, a responsorial psalm, the Gospel, and a homily. "The word of God listened to in common has remarkable effect as compared to its individual reading and better emphasizes the ecclesial character of conversion and reconciliation" (RaP, 32). This form of the sacrament manifests the continuity between the New Covenant in Christ and the Old Testament penitential services such as the one described in Nehemiah 9. "It is particularly meaningful at various seasons of the liturgical year and in connection with events of special pastoral importance" (RaP, 32). The RP includes models for such penitential services, including the seasons of Lent and Advent, and celebrations for children, young people, and the sick (Appendix II). Communal services are a profound and humble sign of the penitential nature of the Church, one of the ways that "the people of God become in the world a sign of conversion to God" (RP, 4).

CONCLUSION

The signs and symbols of the Sacrament of Penance and Reconciliation make present the profound mystery of repentance, reconciliation, and resurrection in the life of the penitent.

> The Sacrament of Forgiveness is an efficacious sign of the word, salvific action and presence of Christ the Redeemer. Through the sacrament, Christ prolongs his words of forgiveness in the words of the priest while, at the same time, transforming the attitude of the penitent who recognizes that he is a sinner and asks forgiveness with the intent of expiation and a purpose of amendment. Actualized in the sacrament is the surprise of the prodigal son as his father forgives him and prepares a feast to celebrate the return of his beloved son (cf. Lk 15:22). (PMDM, 24)

The penitent is a sign of the prodigal son returning home, welcomed by his merciful and forgiving father, signified by the priest, and joyfully embraced by his family and friends, signs of the people of God. The contrition, confession, and satisfaction of the penitent are signs of the inner conversion that has led to the joyous return to the Father's house. And the words of the absolution and its accompanying gestures manifest the Father's mercy and compassion. The two forms express both the individual and the communal dimensions of reconciliation, both the lost sheep welcomed by the Good Shepherd and an unfaithful people returning to him who is always faithful. "In God's design the humanity and loving kindness of our Savior have visibly appeared to us, and God uses visible signs to give salvation and to renew the broken covenant" (RP, 6d).

Further Reading

The *Catechism of the Catholic Church* recommends the following Scripture readings as examinations of conscience: Matthew 5–7; Romans 12–15; 1 Corinthians 12–13; Galatians 5, and Ephesians 4–6.

Chapter 6

Penance and Reconciliation: Living the Sacrament

After Adam and Eve sinned in the Garden of Eden and had hidden from the Lord, God called to Adam, "Where are you?" and sought them out (Gen 3:9). Like our first parents, we long for God, but our sins separate us from him, and yet he calls to us and searches for us. "The desire for God is written in the human heart, because man is created by God and for God; and God never ceases to draw man to himself" (CCC, 27). God is always the one asking us, "Where are you?" when in our sinfulness and shame we hide from him, ceaselessly drawing us back into right relationship with him. The liturgy itself proclaims this divine initiative:

> And when through disobedience he had lost your friendship,
> you did not abandon him to the domain of death.
> For you came in mercy to the aid of all,
> so that those who seek might find you.
> Time and again you offered them covenants
> and through the prophets
> taught them to look forward to salvation.
> (RM, Eucharistic Prayer IV)

God never abandons us, but comes in mercy to raise us up and restore us, and he does so time and again. For this reason, writes St. John Paul II, "the most precious result of the forgiveness obtained in the sacrament of penance consists in reconciliation with God, which takes place in the inmost heart of the son who was lost and found again, which every penitent is" (RaP, 31.V). The restoration of this fundamental relationship, however, "leads, as it were, to other reconciliations which repair the breaches caused by sin" (RaP, 31.V). These include reconciliation with the Church, with others, within ourselves, and "with all creation" (RaP, 31.V). The RP expresses the comprehensive nature of reconciliation in a prayer that is at once simple and profound: "May we reach out with joy to grasp your hand and walk more readily in your ways" (RP, 54, second example, conclusion). In this chapter we will look in detail at the different reconciliations brought about by the sacrament.

RECONCILIATION WITH GOD

The need to be in right relationship with God and others is written into our very being. "Man is a relational being. And if his first, fundamental relationship is disturbed—his relationship with God—then nothing else can be truly in order. This is where the priority lies in Jesus' message and ministry: before all else, he wants to point man toward the essence of his malady, and to show him—if you are not healed *there*, then however many good things you may find, you are not truly healed."[1]

The journey of penance is a journey into the heart of the Trinity, for "the sinner who by the grace of a merciful God embraces the way of penance comes back to the Father who 'first loved us' (1 Jn 4:19), to Christ who gave himself up for us (cf. Gal 2:20; Eph 5:25), and to the Holy Spirit who has been poured out on us abundantly (cf. Ti 3:6)" (RP, 5). One of the Prayers of the Penitent has this Trinitarian structure:

> Lord Jesus Christ,
> you are the Lamb of God;
> you take away the sins of the world.
> Through the grace of the Holy Spirit
> restore me to friendship with your Father,
> cleanse me from every stain of sin
> in the blood you shed for me,
> and raise me to new life
> for the glory of your name. (RP, 91)

Through his sacrifice Christ has brought forgiveness and sent the Holy Spirit who unites us in love to the Father. This prayer also includes the petition, "raise me to new life," for the sacrament constitutes "a true 'spiritual resurrection'" in which the penitent regains "the dignity and blessings of the life of the children of God, of which the most precious is friendship with God" (CCC, 1468). The sacrament thus joins us with the Trinity in an intimate and mutual friendship in which we are restored to God's grace and we in turn "love God deeply and commit ourselves completely to him" (RP, 5).

---

1. Benedict XVI, *Jesus of Nazareth: The Infancy Narratives*, trans. Philip J. Whitmore (NY: Image, 2012), 44; italics original.

RECONCILIATION WITH THE CHURCH

Sin damages our relationship with others and thus wounds the Body of Christ. Reconciliation with the Trinity also reconciles us with the Church which is the Body of Christ, "the fullness of the one who fills all things in every way" (Eph 1:23). At times it can be difficult to see how our sin has wounded the Church. The opening prayer below acknowledges this and asks God to "open our eyes to see the evil we have done" and heal the wounded Body of Christ:

> Almighty and merciful God,
> you have brought us together in the name of your Son
> to receive your mercy and grace in our time of need.
> Open our eyes to see the evil we have done.
> Touch our hearts and convert us to yourself.
> Where sin has divided and scattered,
> may your love make one again;
> where sin has brought weakness,
> may your power heal and strengthen;
> where sin has brought death,
> may your Spirit raise to new life.
> Give us a new heart to love you,
> so that our lives may reflect the image of your Son.
> May the world see the glory of Christ
> revealed in your Church,
> and come to know
> that he is the one whom you have sent,
> Jesus Christ, your Son, our Lord. (RP, 99)

As this prayer makes clear, our sin can bring division, separation, and weakness to the Body of Christ, and dim the revelation of Christ's glory in his Church and so hinder those who are seeking the Lord. The penitent is encouraged to pray for the healing of these wounds: "help me to live in perfect unity with my fellow Christians that I may proclaim your saving power to all the world" (RP, 89). And in communal celebrations, we ask the Lord, "Make us living signs of your love for the whole world to see" (RP, 57.2). Signs of division and conflict are all too abundant in our world—confession enables us to be living signs of God's love.

The penitent reveals an important aspect of the Church when he seeks to heal the wound he has inflicted on the Body of Christ. It is part of the mystery of the Church that, because she is at the same time the Body of Christ who is without sin and also comprised of sinners, she "is at the same time holy and in need of cleansing" and so "unceasingly intent on repentance and reform" (RP, 3). Penance is "the liturgy of the Church's continual self-renewal" (RP, 11). Whenever she celebrates the Sacrament of Penance, "the Church proclaims its faith, gives thanks to God for the freedom with which Christ has made us free, and offers its life as a spiritual sacrifice in praise of God's glory, as it hastens to meet the Lord Jesus" (RP, 7). Reconciliation with the Church also revitalizes the Church, for the sacrament reestablishes or strengthens the penitent's participation in the communion of saints, so that "the sinner is made stronger by the exchange of spiritual goods among all the living members of the Body of Christ, whether still on pilgrimage or already in the heavenly homeland" (CCC, 1469).

PEACE, SERENITY, AND CONSOLATION

When the penitent comes to the sacrament "with contrite heart and religious disposition, reconciliation 'is usually followed by peace and serenity of conscience with strong spiritual consolation'" (CCC, 1468). This peace is woven through the sacramental celebration. The options for welcoming the penitent are invitations to quiet trust and peace: "Come before him with trust in his mercy" (Ezk 33:11); "Have confidence in him" (Lk 5:32); "May the grace of the Holy Spirit fill your heart with light, that you may confess your sins with loving trust and come to know that God is merciful" (RP, 69). One of the options for the act of contrition encourages the penitent to ask for this peace: " . . . May your peace take root in my heart and bring forth a harvest of love, holiness, and truth" (RP, 90). Finally, the options which conclude the celebration again highlight this aspect: "The Lord has freed you from your sins. Go in peace"; " . . . Rejoice in the Lord, and go in peace"; "Go in peace, and proclaim to the world the wonderful works of God, who has brought you salvation" (RP, 47). Whenever the sacrament is celebrated, penitents "experience and proclaim the mercy of God in their own life" (RP, 11).

On the night he was betrayed, Jesus told his disciples, "Peace I leave with you; my peace I give you. Not as the world gives do I give it to you. Do not let your hearts be troubled or afraid" (Jn 14:27).[2] St. Thomas Aquinas, commenting on this verse, described peace as "nothing else than the tranquility arising from order, for things are said to have peace when their order remains undisturbed. In a human being there is a threefold order: that of a person to himself; of a person to God; and of a person to his neighbor. Thus, the human person can enjoy a threefold peace. One peace is interior, when he is at peace with himself, and his faculties are not unsettled: 'Great peace have those who love your law' (Ps 118:165). Another peace is peace with God, when one is entirely conformed to his direction: 'Since we are justified by faith, let us have peace with God' (Rom 5:1). The third peace is with our neighbor: 'Strive for peace with all men' (Heb 12:14)."[3] Reconciliation brings peace, a peace that results from the different reconciliations that flow from reconciliation with God—reconciliation with self, with others, and with all of creation. When we celebrate the sacrament, we are "living a salvific event capable of inspiring fresh life and giving true peace of heart" (RaP, 32).

SPIRITUAL STRENGTH FOR THE CHRISTIAN BATTLE

The grace of the sacrament also confers "an increase of spiritual strength for the Christian battle" (CCC, 1496). Pope Blessed Paul VI described the manifold ways in which the Sacrament of Penance strengthens the penitent: "By it genuine self-knowledge is increased, Christian humility grows, bad habits are corrected, spiritual neglect and tepidity are resisted, the conscience is purified, the will strengthened, a salutary self-control is attained, and grace is increased in virtue of the Sacrament itself" (Mystici Corporis, 88). The saints have much to

---

2. These words are familiar to us from the Mass—after the Our Father the priest says, "Lord Jesus Christ, who said to your Apostles: Peace I leave you, my peace I give, look not on our sins, but on the faith of your Church, and graciously grant her peace and unity in accordance with your will" (RM, Order of Mass, 126). These words are followed by the Sign of Peace and prepare us for sacramental communion.

3. St. Thomas Aquinas, Commentary on the Gospel of John, Chapters 13–21, trans. Fabian Larcher, OP, and James A. Weisheipl, OP (Washington, DC: The Catholic University of America Press, 2010), 88–89.

say about these virtues. Abba Anthony, one of the desert fathers, described the power of humility in the Christian battle: "I saw all the snares of the enemy spread out over the world and groaned saying, 'What can get through such traps?' I heard a voice saying to me, 'Humility.'"[4] Humility, in turn, is born of self-knowledge, as St. Bernard of Clairvaux explained: "But if we are ignorant of God how can we hope in one we do not know? If ignorant about ourselves, how can we be humble, thinking ourselves to be something when we are really nothing?"[5] The power of humility explains the enemy's attempts to hinder its acquisition, as St. Teresa of Avila so well understood: "Terrible are the wiles and deceits used by the devil so that souls may not know themselves or understand their own paths."[6]

Also essential to victory in the Christian battle is the development of spiritual discernment. The Letter to the Hebrews describes mature Christians as "those whose faculties are trained by practice to discern good and evil" (Heb 5:14). Regular confession, even of venial sins, helps us develop this ability, for it "helps us form our conscience, fight against evil tendencies, let ourselves be healed by Christ and progress in the life of the Spirit" (CCC, 1458). In *The Dialogue*, St. Catherine of Siena recorded the Lord's description of how discernment enables the Christian to "fight against evil tendencies" (CCC, 1458): "Discernment . . . has a prudence that cannot be deceived, a strength that is invincible, a constancy right up to the end, reaching as it does from heaven to earth, that is, from the knowledge of me [God] to the knowledge of oneself, from love of me to love of one's neighbors. Discernment's truly humble prudence evades every devilish and creaturely snare, and with unarmed hand—that is, through suffering—it overcomes the devil and the flesh."[7] Discernment is intimately linked to other virtues, as St. Catherine of Siena explains: "For discernment and charity are engrafted together and planted in the soil of that true

---

4. André Louf, OCSO, *The Way of Humility*, trans. Lawrence S. Cunningham (Kalamazoo, MI: Cistercian Publications, 2007), 30.

5. Bernard of Clairvaux, *On the Song of Songs*, II, Sermons 21–46, (Kalamazoo, MI: Cistercian Publications, 1976), 182.

6. St. Teresa of Avila, *The Collected Works*, vol. 2 (Washington, DC: ICS Publications, 1980), 293.

7. Catherine of Siena, *The Dialogue*, The Classics of Western Spirituality (New York: Paulist Press, 1980), 40–41.

humility which is born of self-knowledge."[8] The grace of the sacrament conforms the faithful "more closely to Christ" and makes them "more docile to the voice of the Spirit" (RaP, 32). Cultivating spiritual discernment and docility to the Spirit enables us to "progress in the life of the Spirit" (CCC, 1458).

REDISCOVERING ONE'S TRUE IDENTITY

Original sin introduced a fundamental disorder into every human heart. "Men and women . . . raised themselves up against God, and tried to attain their goal apart from him. . . . When people look into their own hearts they find that they are drawn towards what is wrong and are sunk in many evils which cannot have come from their good creator. Often refusing to acknowledge God as their source, men and women have also upset the relationship which should link them to their final destiny; and at the same time they have broken the right order that should exist within themselves as well as between them and other people and all creatures" (GS, 13). In his Letter to the Romans, the Apostle Paul described his own experience of this interior disorder and disruption: "What I do, I do not understand. For I do not do what I want, but I do what I hate" (Rom 7:15). Our own experience confirms the truth of St. Paul's words.

The Second Vatican Council concisely summarized this intrinsic disorder, affirming that all "are therefore divided interiorly" (GS, 13). This inner division affects all aspects of human life, which "shows itself to be a struggle, and a dramatic one, between good and evil, between light and darkness" (GS, 13). We realize that we are "unable of [our] selves to overcome the assaults of evil successfully, so that everyone feels as if in chains" (GS, 13). "For sin diminished humanity, preventing it from attaining its fulfillment" (GS, 13). Christ came to heal the disorder that reigns in our hearts, "to free and strengthen humanity, renewing it inwardly and casting out that 'prince of this world' (Jn 12:31), who held it in the bondage of sin" (GS, 13).

Christ continues to grant us this freedom, strengthening and renewing us through the Sacrament of Penance, meeting us as the merciful and faithful high priest (Heb 2:17) when we approach him with

---

8. Ibid.

true contrition and sincere conversion. St. John Paul II encouraged us "to recall and emphasize the fact that contrition and conversion are even more a drawing near to the holiness of God, a rediscovery of one's true identity, which has been upset and disturbed by sin, a liberation in the very depth of self and thus a regaining of lost joy, the joy of being saved, which the majority of people in our time are no longer capable of experiencing" (RaP, 31.III). Joy, St. John Paul II teaches us, is not to be found "out there"; rather, it is the fruit of rediscovering our true self, of healing the inner division which we all experience, the experience, to paraphrase St. Paul, of doing the very thing we do not want to do.

ETERNAL AND TEMPORAL PUNISHMENT FOR SIN

Sin has two consequences. These consequences are not "a kind of vengeance inflicted by God from without" but are consequences that follow "from the very nature of sin" (CCC, 1472). The first consequence is the loss of eternal life. Grave or mortal sin breaks our communion with God and so "makes us incapable of eternal life"—this loss of eternal life "is called the 'eternal punishment' of sin" (CCC, 1472). The remedy for this consequence is sacramental confession. The second consequence results from the fact that both grave and venial sin produce "an unhealthy attachment to creatures, which must be purified either here on earth, or after death in the state called Purgatory" (CCC, 1472). This is called the "temporal punishment" of sin. God has also provided a remedy for this consequence—indulgences. The Church's teaching and practice of indulgences is linked to this second consequence, the "temporal punishment" of sin.

The Second Vatican Council produced a beautiful explanation of the doctrine of indulgences in its *Apostolic Constitution on the Revision of Indulgences, Indulgentiarum Doctrina* (*The Doctrine of Indulgences* [ID]). God, in his holiness and justice, requires that sin be punished in order to purify our souls, to defend the holiness of the moral order, and to restore the glory of God "to its full majesty" (ID, 2). Sin "must be expiated either on this earth through the sorrows, miseries and calamities of this life and above all through death, or else in the life beyond through fire and torments or 'purifying' punishments" (ID, 2). All of the harmful effects of sin—to the individual, to social values, and to the universal order—must be healed and the right order restored, "from which there will shine forth throughout the world the sanctity and the splendor of his glory" (ID, 3).

Furthermore, God has established "a supernatural solidarity" among all humanity so that "the sin of one harms others just as the holiness of one also benefits others" (ID, 4). An example of this solidarity is Adam, "whose sin is passed on through propagation to all men. But of this supernatural solidarity the greatest and most perfect principle, foundation and example is Christ himself to communion with Whom God has called us" (ID, 4). His example has taught all Christians to help one another on their journey to the Father "through prayer, the exchange of spiritual goods and penitential expiation" (ID, 5). The more the saints have experienced the love of Christ, the more they have sought to imitate him in his sufferings in the certainty that they can help their brothers and sisters in Christ "to obtain salvation from God the Father of mercies" (ID, 5). The Church calls this "the Communion of the Saints, whereby the life of each individual son of God in Christ and through Christ is joined by a wonderful link to the life of all his other Christian brothers in the supernatural unity of the Mystical Body of Christ till, as it were, a single mystical person is formed" (ID, 5).

All Christians, united to one another through Christ, share in the treasury of the Church "the infinite and inexhaustible value the expiation and the merits of Christ Our Lord have before God, offered as they were so that all of mankind could be set free from sin and attain communion with the Father" (ID, 5). This treasury includes the prayers and good works of the Blessed Virgin Mary and all the saints so that, "while attaining their own salvation, they have also cooperated in the salvation of their brothers in the unity of the Mystical Body" (ID, 5). However, when we speak of the merits of the saints—their prayers and good works—we always refer them to Christ. "*The charity of Christ is the source in us of all our merits* before God. Grace, by uniting us to Christ in active love, ensures the supernatural quality of our acts and consequently their merit before God and before men" (CCC, 2011; italics original). The liturgy itself affirms this truth, for example, in one of the prefaces said in Masses on celebrations of saints: "For you are praised in the company of your Saints and, in crowning their merits, you crown your own gifts" (RM, Order of Mass, 66). "The saints have always had a lively awareness that their merits were pure grace" (CCC, 2011).

The Communion of Saints, whose source and summit is the resurrected and glorified body of Christ, transcends time and space. This means that through the supernatural solidarity of the communion of saints, our communion with those who have gone before us "is not in the least weakened or interrupted, but on the contrary, according to the perpetual faith of the Church, is strengthened by a communication of spiritual goods" (ID, 5). Closely united with Christ in heaven, the saints "establish the whole Church more firmly in holiness, lend nobility to the worship which the Church offers to God here on earth and in many ways contribute to building it up evermore (1 Cor 12:12–27)" (ID, 5). There is a real and intimate union between the saints in heaven, those being purified in purgatory, and the faithful on earth, "a perennial link of charity and an abundant exchange of all the goods by which, with the expiation of all the sins of the entire Mystical Body, divine justice is placated. God's mercy is thus led to forgiveness, so that sincerely repentant sinners may participate as soon as possible in the full enjoyment of the benefits of the family of God" (ID, 5).

The Church, reflecting on these truths under the guidance of the Holy Spirit, has discerned and articulated the doctrine of indulgences, which is "a progression in the doctrine and discipline of the Church rather than a change. From the roots of revelation a new advantage grew in benefit to the faithful and the entire Church" (ID, 7). The ID defines an indulgence as "the remission of the temporal punishment due for sins already forgiven insofar as their guilt is concerned" (ID, 8). In granting an indulgence, the Church, "making use of its power as minister of the Redemption of Christ, not only prays but by an authoritative intervention dispenses to the faithful suitably disposed the treasury of satisfaction which Christ and the saints won for the remission of temporal punishment" (ID, 8). It does so for two reasons: to help the faithful "expiate the punishment due to sin," and to encourage them "to perform works of piety, penitence and charity—particularly those which lead to growth in faith and which favor the common good" (ID, 8). The temporal punishment of sin "must be fulfilled either in the present life or in the world to come, namely in Purgatory. An indulgence offers the penitent sinner the means of discharging this debt during his life on earth."[9]

---

9. Haffner, *The Sacramental Mystery*, 164.

There are two kinds of indulgences, partial and plenary. A partial indulgence removes part of the temporal punishment due to sin, while a plenary indulgence removes all of the temporal punishment due to sin (MI, Norm 2; CCC, 1471). Examples of works which gain a partial indulgence include participating in public novenas, reciting approved litanies with devotion, teaching or studying Christina doctrine, and examining one's conscience with the intention to amend one's life. Examples of works prescribed for a plenary indulgence include visiting the Blessed Sacrament for adoration for at least a half hour; reciting the Rosary in a church, family, association of the faithful, or when several faithful gather; and reading Sacred Scripture for at least a half hour. To gain a plenary indulgence one must, in addition to the prescribed work, be free from all attachment to sin, both grave and venial, and fulfill three conditions: "sacramental confession, Eucharistic Communion, and prayer for the intention of the Sovereign Pontiff" (MI, Norm 20.1). These conditions "may be fulfilled several days before or after the performance of the prescribed work" (MI, Norm 20.3). An indulgence can be gained either for oneself or applied to the dead (MI, Norm 3).

Indulgences benefit the lives of the faithful in numerous ways. They help us grow in humility by reminding us that we cannot remedy the harm caused by our sin through our own efforts. They increase charity by showing "us how closely we are united to each other in Christ" and how we contribute to and benefit from the communion of saints (ID, 9). They rekindle "trust and hope in full reconciliation with God the Father" (ID, 10). Finally, they facilitate the coming of the kingdom of Christ, since through indulgences the "members of the Church who are undergoing purification are united more speedily to those of the Church in heaven" (ID, 10). Indulgences are one of the good gifts of our heavenly Father which he gives us "for our good and the good of all his holy Church" (RM, Order of Mass, 29).

RECONCILIATION WITH ALL CREATION

The final reconciliation, the outer and all-inclusive circle, is reconciliation with all creation (see RaP, 31.V). When we are reconciled with Christ we are reconciled with him "who sustains all things by his

> ## Digging into the Catechism
>
> Read the section on Indulgences in the *Catechism*, nn. 1471–1479. Review these key concepts:
>
> 1. Double consequence of sin (1472)
>
> 2. New man (1473)
>
> 3. Communion of saints (1475)
>
> 4. Wonderful exchange (1475)
>
> 5. Church's treasury (1476)
>
> 6. Binding and loosing (1478)

mighty word" (Heb 1:3), the one in whom "were created all things in heaven and on earth . . . ; all things were created through him and for him" (Col 1:16). There is also an ecclesial dimension to this cosmic reconciliation, for the Church is Christ's body, "the fullness of him who fills all things in every way" (Eph 1:23). In short, all things are summed in Christ, "in heaven and on earth" (Eph 1:10). All creation came into being in, through, and for Christ, is sustained by his word, and is redeemed and moving toward a new heaven and earth through his body the Church. Reconciliation with Christ, with the Trinity, thus has not only a personal dimension, but also a social, an ecclesial, and even a cosmic dimension, rooted ultimately in the mystery of the Word incarnate, "the mystery of God, Christ, in whom are hidden all the treasures of wisdom and knowledge" (Col 2:2–3).

CONCLUSION

The Sacrament of Penance brings about a series of reconciliations that expand in an every widening circle, from the penitent's heart, where the Blessed Trinity dwells, outward to all creation. Our reconciliation with God brings reconciliation with the Body of Christ, the Church. We experience an inner peace and spiritual strength and so rediscover our true self. We are restored to the communion of the saints, and grow in trust, charity, humility, and holiness through the practice of indulgences.

One of the rite's prayers of thanksgiving summarizes the transforming power of this sacrament.

> Lord God,
> creator and ruler of your kingdom of light,
> in your great love for this world
> you gave up your only Son
> for our salvation.
> His cross has redeemed us,
> his death has given us life,
> his resurrection has raised us to glory.
> Through him we ask you
> to be always present among your family.
> Teach us to be reverent in the presence of your glory;
> fill our hearts with faith,
> our days with good works,
> our lives with your love;
> may your truth be on our lips
> and your wisdom in all our actions,
> that we may receive the reward of everlasting life.
> (RP, 208)

This prayer begins by recounting the source of the sacrament's power—the Paschal Mystery—redemption through Christ's Cross, life through his Death, glory through his Resurrection. This paschal power fills us faith, good works, love, truth, and wisdom, gifts which lead us to everlasting life, eternally living within the Trinitarian giving and receiving of the Lover (the Father), the Beloved (the Son), and the Love between them (the Holy Spirit). "We shall, through the healing of our sin, recapture the freshness proper to the Church; we shall rediscover the true face of the Lord, no longer obscured by the idols that our moral conscience and frustrated superego erect; above all, we shall enter into the joy of the Father, as our return gladdens his angels and the communion of saints."[10]

---

10. Corbon, *The Wellspring of Worship*, 170.

PART III:

The Sacrament of
The Anointing of the Sick

Throughout his earthly ministry Jesus showed a special compassion for the sick and suffering. When he sent the Twelve on their first mission, he "gave them authority . . . to cure every disease and every illness" (Mt 10:1). "Even as he had healed every disease and every infirmity," wrote St. Jerome, "he empowered his apostles to heal every disease and every infirmity."[1] Christ's "preferential love for the sick" has never ceased, but "is the source of tireless efforts to comfort them" (CCC, 1502). In this section we will look at how Christ continues to show his preferential love for the sick through the Sacrament of the Anointing of the Sick.

In chapter 7 we will first give a brief overview of the Sacrament of the Anointing of the Sick and then will look in detail at the Old Testament roots of this sacrament. In the Old Testament the sick give voice to their suffering and look to the Lord for healing. Their suffering becomes an occasion for conversion. They also sense that, in a mysterious way, illness is linked to sin and evil. There is an awareness that their suffering can have a redemptive meaning for others. Ultimately, they foresee a time when sickness and suffering will be no more. We will give special attention to passages from the Book of Job and Isaiah's song of the suffering servant (Is 53), and will listen to St. John Paul II's interpretation of these passages.

In chapter 8 we will look at the signs that comprise the sacrament. Two of these sacramental signs symbolize Christ's earthly ministry: the imposition of hands and the Word of Christ that accomplishes what it signifies. Other signs include the prayer of faith and the anointing with the oil of the sick. The participants—the sick, the priest, and the community—constitute another set of signs. Signs like the sign of the Cross, sprinkling with holy

---

1. Manlio Simonetti, ed., *Matthew 1–13*, Ancient Christian Commentary on Scripture, New Testament Ia (Downers Grove, IL: InterVarsity Press, 2001), 191.

113

water, and litanies further enrich the sacrament. And in the celebration of Viaticum, familiar signs acquire new meanings.

Finally, in chapter 9 we will examine the transforming effects of this sacrament. The grace of the Holy Spirit specific to this sacrament confers strength, peace and comfort. It may bring recovery of health if that is beneficial to the sick person's salvation as well as the forgiveness of sin. Another effect is the grace to unite one's sufferings to the Passion of Christ and so contribute to the salvation of the world. The celebration of Viaticum prepares and strengthens the dying for their entrance into eternal life. God, who is rich in mercy (Eph 2:4), richly bestows his grace and mercy on the sick and dying. The Old Testament roots of the Sacrament of the Anointing of the Sick are fulfilled in Christ and prolonged through his Body, the Church, through which he continues to touch and transform the sick and dying.

Chapter 7

Anointing of the Sick: Overview and Old Testament Roots

"Have pity on me, O LORD, for I am languishing, heal me, O LORD, for my body is in terror. My soul, too, is utterly terrified" (Ps 6). This cry of the psalmist expresses a fundamental truth of our existence: "Suffering and illness have always been among the greatest problems that trouble the human spirit" (PCS, 1). This verse also expresses the depths of sickness, for the psalmist's suffering is emotional as well as physical; terror afflicts both his body and his soul. This reveals the nature of the human person. Because each of us is an inseparable unity of body and soul, caring for the sick must address both. In sickness we experience our powerlessness, our limitations, and our finitude, which can lead to "anguish, self-absorption, sometimes even despair and revolt against God" (CCC, 1500–1501). But the psalmist makes his appeal to God by saying, "Have pity on me, O LORD." In so doing, he affirms that his healing ultimately will come only from God: "Heal me, O LORD." In illness we "glimpse death"—a glimpse that can provoke "a search for God and a return to him" (CCC, 1500–1501).

INSTITUTION BY CHRIST

During his earthly ministry, Christ "showed great concern for the bodily and spiritual welfare of the sick" (PCS, 5). He not only healed the paralytic, but first forgave his sin (Mk 2:1–12); he brought freedom to those oppressed by demons (Lk 8:26–39), proclaimed God's ability to do the impossible (Mk 9:23), and comforted their loved ones (Lk 7:13). Such is the depth of Christ's compassion for the sick "that he identifies himself with them: 'I was sick and you visited me'" (CCC, 1503). His healing ministry reveals that "he has come to heal the whole man, soul and body; he is the physician the sick have need of (Mk 2:17)" (CCC, 1503). Even more, Christ's compassion and care for the sick as recorded in the Gospel is "a resplendent sign that 'God has visited his people' and that the Kingdom of God is close at hand" (CCC, 1503).

Christ equipped his disciples to "share in his ministry of compassion and healing" (CCC, 1506). "So they went out and preached that men should repent. And they cast out many demons, and anointed with oil many that were sick and healed them" (Mk 6:12–13). In his earthly ministry Christ instituted the Sacrament of the Anointing of the Sick, and it "is made known in the Letter of James" (PCS, 5). "Is anyone among you sick?" asks James, "he should summon the presbyters of the church, and they should pray over him and anoint [him] with oil in the name of the Lord, and the prayer of faith will save the sick person, and the Lord will raise him up. If he has committed any sins, he will be forgiven" (Jas 5:14–15). "Since then the Church has never ceased to celebrate this sacrament for its members by the anointing and the prayer of its priests, commending those who are ill to the suffering and glorified Lord, that he may raise them up and save them" (PCS, 5).

THE RECIPIENT AND MINISTER

The Second Vatican Council taught that the Anointing of the Sick "is not a sacrament intended only for those who are at the point of death" (SC, 73). It is for "those of the faithful whose health is seriously impaired by sickness or old age" (PCS, 8).[1] The sacrament may be repeated if the person's condition worsens or if he or she "recovers after being anointed and then again falls ill" (PCS, 9). A person who is having surgery for a serious illness may be anointed before the surgery (PCS, 10). Children and the elderly who "have sufficient use of reason to be strengthened by this sacrament" may be anointed (PCS, 11–12). The sacrament may also be conferred on "the elderly whose frailty becomes more pronounced" (CCC, 1515). The faithful who have lost consciousness or the use of reason but who would have "at least implicitly asked for it when they were in control of their faculties" are also to be anointed (PCS, 14). If there is doubt about whether the sick person is

---

1. The word "seriously" is a translation of the Latin *periculose*. The PCS explains the translation and meaning of this word: "The word *periculose* has been carefully studied and rendered as 'seriously,' rather than as 'gravely,' 'dangerously,' or 'perilously.' Such a rendering will serve to avoid restrictions upon the celebration of the sacrament. On the one hand, the sacrament may and should be given to anyone whose health is seriously impaired; on the other hand, it may not be given indiscriminately or to any person whose health is not seriously impaired" (PCS, 8n). The rite stipulates that "a prudent or reasonably sure judgment, without scruple, is sufficient for deciding on the seriousness of an illness; if necessary a doctor may be consulted" (PCS, 8).

dead, the sacrament is to be conferred (PCS, 15). The only proper minister of this sacrament is a priest (bishops and presbyters).

PASTORAL CARE OF THE SICK

The title of the official ritual book for the Anointing of the Sick is *Pastoral Care of the Sick* (PCS). The title itself indicates that the Church's concern for the sick is not limited to the administration of the sacrament of anointing. When Jesus sent the Twelve to preach the Gospel, he told them, "Cure the sick" (Mt 10:8). "The Church has received this charge from the Lord and strives to carry it out by taking care of the sick as well as by accompanying them with her prayer of intercession" (CCC, 1509). The content of the *Pastoral Care of the Sick* reflects this comprehensive concern for the care of the sick.

The PCS is divided into three parts. Part I, "Pastoral Care of the Sick," contains rites that "are used by the Church to comfort the sick in time of anxiety, to encourage them to fight against illness, and perhaps to restore them to health" (PCS, 42). It includes rites for "Visits to the Sick" (chapter 1), "Visits to a Sick Child" (chapter 2), "Communion of the Sick" (chapter 3), and "Anointing of the Sick" (chapter 4)—the administration of the sacrament. The different rites found in this chapter affirm that care for the sick "is the common responsibility of all Christians, who should visit the sick, remember them in prayer, and celebrate the sacraments with them" (PCS, 43).

Entitled "Pastoral Care of the Dying," part II of the PCS contains rites that "are used by the Church to comfort and strengthen a dying Christian in the passage from this life" (PCS, 161). Care for the dying "places emphasis on trust in the Lord's promise of eternal life rather than on the struggle against illness which is characteristic of the pastoral care of sick [part I] (PCS, 161). The first three chapters of this section—"Celebration of Viaticum", "Commendation of the Dying", "Prayers for the Dead"—"provide for those situations in which time is not a pressing concern and the rites can be celebrated fully and properly" (PCS, 161). The final chapter, "Rites for Exceptional Circumstances", contains rites "for emergency circumstances and should be used only when such pressing conditions exist" (PCS, 166). Although there is no special rite for the care of a dying child, the introduction to this section includes suggestions "to help bring into focus the various aspects of this ministry" (PCS, 168). The final section is a compendium of readings, responses and verses from Sacred Scripture.

The variety of rites contained in the PCS witnesses to the truth that the Lord's "preferential love for the sick has not ceased through the centuries to draw the very special attention of Christians toward all those who suffer in body and soul. It is the source of tireless efforts to comfort them" (CCC, 1503). The Church's care and concern for the sick brings blessings to both the sick and those who care for them, as Pope Benedict XVI noted in *The Sacrament of Charity*: "Attentive pastoral care shown to those who are ill brings great spiritual benefit to the entire community, since whatever we do to one of the least of our brothers and sisters, we do to Jesus himself (cf. Mt 25:40)" (SacCar, 22).

CELEBRATION OF THE SACRAMENT

The structure of the Sacrament of the Anointing of the Sick varies depending on whether it is celebrated within Mass or outside of Mass (in the home, in a hospital or institution, or in church). The latter has the simplest form and so reveals the essential structure of the sacrament. It begins with the Introductory Rites—a brief greeting and preparatory instruction. This is followed by the Liturgy of Anointing: the laying on of hands, anointing with the Oil of the Sick, the Lord's Prayer, and the Prayer after Anointing. It concludes with a blessing. The rite for celebration outside of Mass expands this basic structure in a couple of ways. The Introductory Rites include sprinkling with holy water and a penitential rite, and the Liturgy of Anointing is preceded by a Liturgy of the Word. This can then be followed by Communion before concluding with the final blessing. The chart on the next page compares the two rites.

The sacrament is comprised of three principal elements: "the 'priests of the Church'—in silence—lay hands on the sick; they pray over them in the faith of the Church—this is the epiclesis proper to this sacrament; they then anoint them with oil blessed, if possible, by the bishop" (CCC, 1519). The priest usually anoints the forehead and the hands of the sick, although the PCS allows for the anointing of other parts of the body such as the area of injury or pain, "depending upon the culture and traditions of the place, as well as the condition of the sick person" (PCS, 124). The anointing is accompanied by the essential

Anointing in a Hospital or Institution (PCS, 153)	Anointing Outside of Mass (PCS, 114)
Introductory Rites	Introductory Rites
Greeting	Song
Instruction	Greeting
	Introduction
	Opening Prayer
	Liturgy of the Word
	Reading
	Response
Liturgy of Anointing	Liturgy of Anointing
Laying on of Hands	Litany
Anointing	Laying on of Hands
The Lord's Prayer	Prayer over the Oil
Prayer after Anointing	Anointing
	Prayer after Anointing
	The Lord's Prayer
	[Liturgy of Holy Communion]
	Communion
	Silent Prayer
	Prayer after Communion
Concluding Rite	Concluding Rite
Blessing	Blessing
Proclamation of Praise of God and Dismissal	

words (the form) of the sacrament. The priest anoints the forehead of the sick person while saying, "Through this holy anointing may the Lord in his love and mercy help you with the grace of the Holy Spirit" (PCS, 124). He then anoints the hands and says, "May the Lord who frees you from sin save you and raise you up" (PCS, 124).

IN THE PRESENCE OF GOD

The Old Testament reveals many facets of sickness and healing, for "the man of the Old Testament lives his sickness in the presence of God" (CCC, 1502). The summary in the *Catechism* suggests five different aspects of the sacrament that are expressed by the man of the Old Testament. First, he "laments his illness" and "implores healing" from God (CCC, 1502), as we hear in Psalm 38: "Foul and festering are my sores because of my folly. . . . My loins burn with fever; there is no wholesomeness in my flesh. . . . LORD, it is for you that I wait; O Lord, my God, you respond. . . . I am very near to falling; my wounds are with me always. . . . Come quickly to help me, my Lord and my salvation!" (Ps 38:6, 8, 16, 23). It is to the Lord that he recounts his suffering and from the Lord begs healing and salvation.

Lamentation, prayer and response are present in the illness of King Hezekiah as described in Isaiah 38. "In those days, when Hezekiah was mortally ill, the prophet Isaiah, son of Amoz, came and said to him: 'Thus says the LORD: Put your house in order, for you are about to die; you shall not recover.' Hezekiah turned his face to the wall and prayed to the LORD: 'Ah, LORD, remember how faithfully and wholeheartedly I conducted myself in your presence, doing what was good in your sight'" (Is 38:1–3). After Hezekiah had heard Isaiah's prophecy, St. Cyril of Jerusalem wonders, "What expectation was left? What hope of recovery was there?" He continues, "But Hezekiah remembered what was written—'In the hour that you turn and lament, you will be saved.' He turned his face to the wall, and from his bed of pain his mind soared up to heaven (for no wall is so thick as to stifle fervent prayer). He said, 'Lord, remember me.' . . . He whom the prophet's sentence had forbidden to hope was granted further years of life, the sun turning back its course as a witness."[2]

A second aspect of the man of the Old Testament living his sickness before God is that illness can become a way to conversion. Concerning King Hezekiah, St. Cyril of Jerusalem writes, "Do you want to know the power of repentance? Do you want to understand this strong weapon of salvation and the might of confession? . . . The same king's repentance won the repeal the sentence God had passed on

---

2. Steven A. McKinion, ed., *Isaiah 1–39*, Ancient Christian Commentary on Scripture, Old Testament X (Downers Grove, IL: InterVaristy Press, 2004), 262.

him."[3] Furthermore, "God's forgiveness initiates healing" (CCC, 1502), as we see in Psalm 107: "Some fell sick from their wicked ways, afflicted because of their sins. They loathed all manner of food; they were at the gates of death. In their distress they cried to the LORD, who saved them in their peril, sent forth his word to heal them, and snatched them from the grave" (Ps 107:17–20). Sin can lead to sickness, repentance to forgiveness and healing.

A third aspect is the relationship between illness and sin. "It is the experience of Israel that illness is mysteriously linked to sin and evil, and that faithfulness to God according to his law restores life" (CCC, 1502).[4] The first trial that Israel encountered during its wilderness wanderings was the spring of bitter water at Marah (Ex 15:22 ff.). Moses besought the Lord, who instructed him to throw into the water a piece of wood, and "the water became fresh" (Ex 15:25). The narrator tells us that here God "put them to the test. He said: 'If you listen closely to the voice of the LORD, your God, and do what is right in his eyes: if you heed his commandments and keep his statutes, I will not afflict you with any of the diseases with which I afflicted the Egyptians; for I, the LORD, am your healer'" (Ex 15:26). This first trial is a deliberate allusion to the first Egyptian plague, the blood waters. The lesson is clear: "If Israel opens its heart, then its fate will be different from the Egyptians' for it will experience Yahweh as healer (v. 26) rather than sender of plagues."[5]

Fourth, the man of the Old Testament also understood that suffering can also have a redemptive meaning for the sins of others. This is clearly expressed in Isaiah 53: "My servant, the just one, shall justify the many, their iniquity he shall bear" (Is 53:11). We will discuss this passage in detail later in this chapter. Fifth, a time will come when God "will pardon every offense and heal every illness" (CCC, 1502). In a future Jerusalem, Isaiah prophesies that "no one who dwells there will say, 'I am sick'; the people who live there will be forgiven their guilt" (Is 33:24). Commenting of this

---

3. Ibid., 261.

4. We should note, however, that the Church does not teach that all sickness is a result of sin, as St. John Paul II has noted: "*It is not true* that *all suffering is a consequence of a fault and has the nature of punishment*" (SD, 11, italics original). When Jesus and his disciples pass a man born blind, his disciples ask him who sinned, the man or his parents, "that he was born blind?" Jesus replied that the man's blindness was not the result of sin, "but that the works of God might be made manifest in him" (Jn 9:2–3).

5. Brown et al., *New Jerome Biblical Commentary*, 50.

prophecy of salvation, Clement of Alexandria writes, "This is the greatest and noblest of all God's acts: saving humanity. But those who labor under some sickness are dissatisfied if the physician prescribes no remedy to restore their health. How, then, can we withhold our sincerest gratitude from the divine Educator when he corrects the acts of disobedience that sweep us on to ruin and uproots the desires that drag us into sin, refusing to be silent and connive at them, and even offers counsels on the right way to live? Certainly we owe him the deepest gratitude."[6]

The Old Testament illuminates some of the fundamental aspects of sickness and anticipates the definitive healing of body and soul—salvation—that Christ will accomplish through the Paschal Mystery.

READINGS

Pope Benedict XVI described the power of the Word of God in the celebration of this sacrament. "It must not be forgotten that 'the healing power of the word of God is a constant call to the listener's personal conversion.' Sacred Scripture contains countless pages which speak of the consolation, support, and healing which God brings. We can think particularly of Jesus' own closeness to those who suffer, and how he, God's incarnate Word, shouldered our pain and suffered out of love for us, thus giving meaning to sickness and death" (VD, 61). Christ is truly present in his Word, through which he still comforts, supports and heals his children. The PCS offers a number of different Old Testament passages for use in the celebration of the sacrament. It encourages ministers to consider the particular conditions of the sick when selecting readings: "The selection [of readings] should be made according to pastoral need, and special attention should be given to the physical and spiritual condition of the sick persons for whom the readings are used" (PCS, 297). We will look at several passages from Job as well as Isaiah 52:13—53:12.

WHEN SHALL I ARISE?

Job, one of the Wisdom books, "is an exquisite dramatic treatment of the problem of the suffering of the innocent. The contents of the book, together with its artistic structure and elegant style, place it among the

---

6. McKinion, ed. *Isaiah 1–39*, 234.

literary masterpieces of all time. This is a literary composition, and not a transcript of historical events and conversations."[7] The book begins with the Lord allowing Satan to visit a series of catastrophes on Job. Three of his friends come to console him, and a cycle of speeches among them follows, Job insisting on his innocence and his friends equally insistent that his suffering is the result of sin. They are joined later by a young bystander who supports the view of Job's friends. The poem concludes with an extended address by God to Job on the mystery and wonders of God's work in creation. God settles the debate between Job and his friends, telling the friends, "You have not spoken rightly concerning me, as has my servant Job" (42:7). The Lord then "blessed the latter days of Job more than his earlier ones" (42:12).

The first selection comes from chapter 3, in which Job laments the suffering that has befallen him—the death of his children and his servants and the loss of his livestock, after which he is afflicted "with severe boils from the soles of his feet to the crown of his head" (2:7). "Perish the day on which I was born," he begins (3:3). Then he continues with a series of questions: "Why did I not perish at birth, come forth from the womb and expire?" (v. 11); "Wherefore did the knees receive me?" (v. 12); "Why is light given to the toilers, and life to the bitter in spirit?" (v. 20). He concludes, "They wait for death . . . rejoice in it exultingly, and are glad when they reach the grave" (vv. 21–22), for they are "men whose path is hidden from them, and whom God has hemmed in!" (v. 23). In Job's words we hear the "anguish, self-absorption, sometimes even despair and revolt against God" (CCC, 1500–1501), and even "bewilderment about God's goodness" that can overwhelm the sick.[8]

The next passage is Job 7:1–4, 6–11 in which we hear Job's inner anguish, turmoil and despair. He sees life as "a drudgery" (v. 1), himself as "a hireling" and "a slave" (v. 2), one who has "been assigned months of misery" (v. 3). Sleep eludes him: "If in bed . . . the night drags on" and he is "filled with restlessness until the dawn" (v. 4). His life now "is like the wind", like "a cloud that dissolves and vanishes" (v. 7, 9). "My own utterance I will not restrain; I will speak in the anguish of my spirit; I will complain in the bitterness of my soul" (v. 11). In this passage, "Job,

---

7. *New American Bible*, 596.

8. Brown et al., *New Jerome Biblical Commentary*, 471.

accustomed to an untroubled relationship with his divine benefactor, appeals implicitly to the love God has for him. His human friends have failed him, but he takes for granted that his divine friend will come looking for him—only it may be too late."[9] This kind of passage can help the sick to express their own feelings and fears about their illness.

The remainder of this chapter, 7:12–21, is the next reading. Job continues his complaint about his life, but now in a series of statements and questions addressed to God: "Job's first formal prayer"[10]; "why should you set me up as an object of attack? or why should I be a target for you?" (v. 12); "you affright me with dreams, and with visions terrify me" (v. 14). "Let me alone," he pleads, "for my days are but a breath" (v. 16). The questions pour out of his soul: "What is man, that you make much of him, or pay him any heed?" (v. 17); "how long will it be before you look away from me, and let me alone long enough to swallow my spittle?" (v. 19); "though I have sinned, what can I do to you, O watcher of men? Why do you not pardon my offense, or take away my guilt?" (v. 20–21). God, whom Job has known "as a person adored and loved, whom he can address intimately . . . has now turned on Job, maltreating and tormenting him."[11] The question Job—and perhaps the sick person today—struggles with is, "Why is a friend suddenly acting like a vicious enemy?"[12]

The final passage from Job is 19:23–27, which is recommended for the dying (PCS, 157). In this familiar passage, Job's faith shines forth: "I know that my Vindicator[13] lives, and that he will at last stand forth upon the dust" (v. 25). He believes in him "whom I myself shall see: my own eyes, not another's, shall behold him. And from my flesh I shall see God" (v. 25–27). "This sight of God, emphasized three times, is what Job really craves."[14] Israelite belief held "that Yahweh was 'the living God,' and this dynamism seems to provide a connection of thought with Job's 'survival of consciousness' after death. The divine vitality is such that it

---

9. Ibid., 473.

10. Ibid.

11. Ibid.

12. Ibid.

13. "Vindicator" in Hebrew is *go'el* and "means the next of kin whose obligation it was to rescue from poverty, redeem from slavery, or avenge a death" (Brown et al., *New Jerome Biblical Commentary*, 478). "It is often used of God, the Savior of his people and avenger of the oppressed" (*New Jerusalem Bible*, 779, note g).

14. Brown et al., *New Jerome Biblical Commentary*, 478.

will cause Job, even in the underworld, to have at least momentary knowledge, or rather vision, of what occurs on earth."[15] For a moment, eternity breaks into time, faith transcends sense: "Job's faith thus momentarily defies horizons of mortality in his desperate need for justice; it prepares us for the explicit revelation of bodily resurrection."[16]

St. John Paul II discusses the book of Job in his apostolic letter, *On the Christian Meaning of Human Suffering*. "The book of Job poses in an extremely acute way the question of the 'why' of suffering" (SD, 12), especially the assertion that all suffering is punishment for sin. St. John Paul II explains:

> Job however challenges the truth of the principle that identifies suffering with punishment for sin. And he does this on the basis of his own opinion. For he is aware that he has not deserved such punishment, and in fact he speaks of the good that he has done during his life. In the end, God himself reproves Job's friends for their accusations and recognizes that Job is not guilty. His suffering is the suffering of someone who is innocent and it must be accepted as a mystery, which the individual is unable to penetrate completely by his own intelligence. (SD, 11)

This is an important point to note, both for those who suffer and those who care for them. Job cautions us against offering a glib explanation for what is in fact a profound mystery.

THE SUFFERING SERVANT

The Song of the Suffering Servant, Isaiah 52:13—53:12, is another Old Testament option. It comes from the section of Isaiah known as Second Isaiah, chapters 40–55. While chapters 1–39 of Isaiah call Israel to repentance and warn of judgment, chapters 40–55 address a very different situation. Known as the Book of Comfort from the opening words of Isaiah 40:1—"Comfort, give comfort to my people, says your God"—Second Isaiah is addressing a defeated nation taken into exile in Babylon. The author is speaking to "a people discouraged, dazed, and destitute, severely tempted to apostasy. The people in exile must be consoled, not punished; their faith must be sustained, not further tried."[17] The Four Songs of the Servant Yahweh (42:1–7; 49:1–7; 50:4–9;

---

15. Ibid..

16. *New Jerusalem Bible*, 779, note g.

17. Brown et al., *New Jerome Biblical Commentary*, 330.

52:13—53:12) are jewels of Second Isaiah, poems that "depict a perfect servant of Yahweh—re-gatherer of his people and light of nations—one who preaches the true faith, who expiates the people's sins by his own death and is glorified by God."[18] Let us now look at the Fourth Song.

The passage begins with the exaltation of the servant: "See, my servant shall prosper, he shall be raised high and greatly exalted" (52:13). He will, however, amaze many, startle nations, and render kings speechless, "so marred was his look beyond that of mortals" (52:14–15). Then begins the account of his sorrows. "He was spurned and avoided by men, a man of suffering, accustomed to infirmity, one of those from whom men hide their faces, spurned, and he held him in no esteem" (53:3). The servant endures "a bitter sense of loneliness. The servant relives the persecuted role of Jeremiah (15:17) and Job (19:13–19)."[19]

Yet his sufferings and sorrow were part of his ministry, for "it was our infirmities that he bore, our sufferings that he endured. . . . He was pierced for our offenses, crushed for our sins; upon him was the chastisement that makes us whole, by his stripes we were healed" (Is 53:4–5). The reference to chastisement "recalls the disciplinary or educative power of suffering. God teaches repentance through the calamity evoked by sin."[20] Here we encounter the redemptive meaning of suffering that will find its fulfillment on the Cross.

Although the people had gone astray, "each following his own way," the Lord placed on him "the guilt of us all" (53:6). "The servant . . . is not freeing others of their responsibility for repentance but is suffusing within them his own spirit of sorrow and hope."[21] The servant silently accepts his sufferings: "Like a lamb led to the slaughter . . . he was silent and opened not his mouth" (53:7). He is then taken away, "after being seized, tried, and convicted . . . psychologically into a loneliness almost to the point of despair."[22] His suffering for others is reiterated: he was "smitten for the sin of his people" (53:8); "he gives his life as an offering for sin" (53:10). Also reiterated is

---

18. *New Jerusalem Bible*, 1169.

19. Brown et al., *New Jerome Biblical Commentary*, 342.

20. Ibid.

21. Ibid., 342.

22. Ibid.

the fact that he suffers innocently, for "he had done no wrong nor spoken any falsehood" (53:9).

The passage closes with a description of the fruits of the servant's sufferings. "Through his suffering, my servant shall justify many, and their guilt he shall bear" (53:11). This is a particularly rich verse. "Through his suffering" can also be translated "by his knowledge" (Hebrew), which means "by a full experiential union with a suffering, sinful people."[23] The justification of many means that "he will share his own goodness with them and thus fulfill all divine promises."[24] This servant who has suffered innocently "shall see the light in fullness of days" (53:11) and grant to his descendants "a long life" (53:10), accomplishing in his own life "the will of the Lord" (53:10). The mystery of the suffering servant is profound, for "the servant remains one with all people in sorrow and yet distinct from them in innocence of life and total service of God. The doctrine of expiatory suffering finds supreme expression (vv. 4, 6, 10)."[25]

While the passages regarding the servant's suffering were excluded from Jewish messianic theology, these "were the very ones which Jesus emphasized, applying them to himself and his mission, Mk 10:45; Lk 22:19–20, 37, while earliest Christian preaching identified him as the perfect Servant foretold by Second Isaiah, Mt 12:17–21; Jn 1:29."[26] In this passage, writes St. John Paul II, "the passion of Christ becomes almost more expressive and touching than in the descriptions of the evangelists themselves" (SD, 17). When Christ declares on the Cross, "It is finished" (Jn 19:30), we know

> that the Scripture has been fulfilled, that these words of the Song of the Suffering Servant have been definitively accomplished: "It was the will of the Lord to bruise him" (Is 53:10). Human suffering has reached its culmination in the Passion of Christ. And at the same time it has entered into a completely new dimension and a new order: *it has been linked to love,* to that love of which Christ spoke to Nicodemus, to that love that creates good, drawing it out by means of suffering, just as the supreme good of the Redemption of the world was drawn from the Cross of Christ, and from that Cross constantly takes its beginning. The Cross of Christ has become a source from which flow rivers of living water (Jn 7:37–38). (SD,18)

---

23. Ibid.
24. Ibid.
25. Ibid., 341
26. *New Jerusalem Bible*, 1170.

The Fourth Servant Song anticipates not only Christ's complete identification with our suffering, but also its transformation through love, creating an infinite and inexhaustible good for the salvation of the world.

FOOD FOR THE JOURNEY

Viaticum, which means "fare, money or provision for a journey,"[27] "is the sacrament proper to the dying Christian. It is the completion and crown of the Christian life on this earth, signifying that the Christian follows the Lord to eternal glory and the banquet of the heavenly kingdom" (PCS, 175). The Sacrament of the Anointing of the Sick is the sacrament proper to "the beginning of a serious illness. Viaticum, celebrated when death is close, will then be better understood as the last sacrament of Christian life" (PCS, 175). The Church suggests two Old Testament passages for the celebration of Viaticum: Job 19:23–27 (discussed above) and 1 Kings 19:4–8, the account of Elijah in the desert.

Elijah has fled to the desert after slaughtering the prophets of Baal who served Jezebel, the wife of King Ahab. Incensed at Elijah's triumph, Jezebel threatens Elijah with revenge: "May the gods do thus to me and more, if by this time tomorrow I have not done with your life what was done to each of them" (1 Kgs 19:2). Alone, discouraged, facing death, he leaves his servant and travels a day's journey into the desert. He sits beneath a broom tree and prays for death: "This is enough, O Lord! Take my life, for I am

---

Digging into the Catechism

Read the *Catechism*'s citations of the Fourth Servant Song. What does each citation reveal about the meaning of this passage?

1. CCC, 713

2. CCC, 601

3. CCC, 615

4. CCC, 608

5. CCC, 627

6. CCC, 623

---

27. Leo F. Stelten, *Dictionary of Ecclesiastical Latin* (Peabody, MA: Hendrickson, 1995), 285.

no better than my fathers" (19.4). He is awakened from sleep by an angel who orders him to get up and eat. By his head he sees a hearth cake and a jug of water, but after eating and drinking he lies down again. The angel returns, touches him, and says, "Get up and eat, else the journey will be too long for you!" He does as the angel commands, and strengthened by the food, walks "forty days and forty nights to the mountain of God, Horeb" (19:8).

In this passage Elijah feels isolated, dejected, abandoned, feelings common to those for whom death is imminent. The Lord sends a messenger to Elijah to nourish and encourage him in body and in soul. In Viaticum the Lord again sends his servant to those facing death, nourishing them with the Body and Blood of Christ so that the journey they are facing will not be too long for them. This brief account speaks powerfully of the struggles that may afflict the dying and of the Lord's compassionate presence and provision.

CONCLUSION

The depiction of illness in the Old Testament anticipates several aspects of suffering. The Old Testament expresses both the despair and hope of the one who suffers, as well as the certainty that healing belongs to God. It acknowledges that illness can be a path to a deeper relationship with God. It wrestles with the connection between illness and sin. It sees the redemptive value of physical suffering, and foresees an end to sickness. The character of Job gives poignant voice to the emotional and physical suffering, but his faith overcomes his temptation to despair. The Suffering Servant vividly depicts the one who suffers for the healing of others. If Job poses the questions about the mystery of suffering, the Suffering Servant offers the prophetic answer that is fulfilled in Christ. Elijah, the powerful but persecuted prophet, is a sign of God's presence and provision for those on their final journey to him. These passages introduce us to the mystery of suffering and healing, and give voice to the feelings and questions of those we are called to care for.

Chapter 8

Anointing of the Sick: Signs and Symbols of the Sacrament

Jesus utilized a variety of signs in his healing ministry, familiar signs and actions such as touch and the laying on of hands, but also surprising and unconventional signs—spittle and mud, even the hem of his garment. All of these signs, the familiar as well as the surprising, are examples of how God, "by invisible power," accomplishes "a wondrous effect through sacramental signs" (RM, Easter Vigil, Blessing of Baptismal Water, 46). Christ's power to heal drew the sick to him. "The sick try to touch him, 'for power came forth from him and healed them all' (Lk 6:19), and so in the sacraments Christ continues to 'touch' us in order to heal us" (CCC, 1504). The Sacrament of the Anointing of the Sick is comprised of a rich variety of signs. Some, like oil, the imposition of hands, and the authoritative and performative word of Christ, we recognize from Jesus' own ministry. The Church, guided by the Holy Spirit, has added other signs: the sign of the cross and sprinkling with holy water. Additionally, even the priest, the sick person, and the community of family and friends are signs of the Lord's saving presence and power.

THE STRUCTURE OF THE SACRAMENT

The chart on page 131, which I introduced in chapter 7, shows two forms of celebrating the sacrament: a simpler form for use in hospitals and institutions and a fuller form which "may be used to anoint a number of people within the same celebration" such as those celebrated in a parish, diocesan gatherings, or for pilgrimages (PCS, 108). In this chapter, I will first look at the signs for the form used in hospitals and institutions, and then discuss some of the additional elements included in the form for use with larger gatherings. There is flexibility when celebrating either form. The PCS allows for a number of adaptations. Recognizing "that the sick tire easily and that their physical condition may change from day to day and even from hour to hour," it permits the shortening of the celebration "if necessary" (PCS, 40). The priest is encouraged to accommodate the structure of the rite "to the place and people involved" (PCS, 41). For example, a penitential rite may be included either in the introductory rite or after the reading of Scripture.

Anointing in a Hospital or Institution (PCS, 153)	Anointing outside of Mass (PCS, 114)
Introductory Rites	Introductory Rites
Greeting	Greeting
Instruction	Sprinkling with Holy Water
	Instruction
	Penitential Rite
	Liturgy of the Word
	Reading
	Response
Liturgy of Anointing	Liturgy of Anointing
Laying on of Hands	Litany
Anointing	Laying On of Hands
The Lord's Prayer	Prayer over the Oil
Prayer after Anointing	Anointing
	Prayer after Anointing
	The Lord's Prayer
	[Liturgy of Holy Communion]
	Communion
	Silent Prayer
	Prayer after Communion
Concluding Rite	Concluding Rite
Blessing	Blessing

In addition to these two forms, "It is very fitting to celebrate it within the Eucharist, the memorial of the Lord's Passover" (CCC, 1517). In this case, the celebration of the sacrament follows the Liturgy of the Word and has the following structure: Litany, Laying On of Hands, Prayer over the Oil, Anointing, and Prayer after Anointing.

THE PRIEST

In the Sacrament of Penance and Reconciliation, the priest as the sacramental representation of Christ makes present the brother of man, the merciful high priest, the shepherd intent on finding the lost sheep, and the physician who heals and comforts (see RaP, 29). In the Sacrament of the Anointing of the Sick, he is "an 'icon' of Christ the priest" (CCC, 1142) who healed those who were sick in body and soul. He makes present Christ who healed the centurion's servant from a distance (Mt 8:1–13); Christ who freed the woman bound by a spirit for eighteen years (Lk 13:10–17); Christ who comforted the widow of Nain whose son had died and whom he raised from the dead (Lk 7:11–17); Christ who, moved by compassion, touched the leper and healed him (Mk 1:40–45); and Christ who asked the blind beggar, "What do you want me to do for you?" and then restored his sight (Mk 10:46–52). In the person of the priest the sick encounter the power and compassion of Christ.

THE SICK PERSON

The recipient of the sacrament can be a powerful sign to the Church and the world. The PCS teaches us that "the role of the sick in the Church is to be a reminder to others of the essential or higher things. By their witness the sick show that our mortal life must be redeemed through the mystery of Christ's death and resurrection" (PCS, 3). In his message for the World Day of the Sick (August 22, 2000), St. John Paul II explained the sign value of the sick. To them he addressed the following words: "Dear brothers and sisters, proclaim and bear witness to the Gospel of life and hope with generous dedication. Proclaim that Christ is the comfort of all who are in distress or difficulty; he is the strength of those experiencing moments of fatigue and vulnerability; he is the support of those who work zealously to assure better living and health conditions for everyone."[1] In a world afflicted by strife and suffering, the sick can speak powerfully to us about the power of friendship with Christ—his comfort, strength, and support.

In this way the sick participate in the new evangelization, which was the theme of the World Day of the Sick in 2001: *The New*

---

1. Accessed August 25, 2014, http://www.vatican.va/holy_father/john_paul_ii /messages/sick/documents/hf_jp-ii_mes_20000822_world-day-of-the-sick-2001_en.html.

Evangelization and the Dignity of the Suffering Person. In this regard, St. John Paul II explained that "the Church intends to stress the need to evangelize in a new way this area of human experience, in order to encourage its orientation to the overall well-being of the person and the progress of all people in every part of the world."[2] Recognizing the sick as signs of Christ's saving power can deepen the faith of the faithful and bring nonbelievers into a saving relationship with the Lord. This sacrament enables the sick to contribute to the salvation of the world: "the Anointing of the Sick, for its part, unites the sick with Christ's self-offering for the salvation of all so that they too, within the mystery of the communion of saints, can participate in the redemption of the world" (SacCar, 22). The recipients of this sacrament are a beautiful sign of the reciprocity of this sacrament, the priest and community caring for the sick, and the sick contributing through their suffering to the faith and salvation of the community and the world.

THE COMMUNITY

Those present for the celebration of the sacrament—family, friends, parishioners, doctors, and nurses—constitute a sign of the universal Church. "The entire Church is made present in this community—represented by at least the priest, family, friends, and others—assembled to pray for those to be anointed. If they are able, the sick persons should also join in this prayer" (PCS, 105). The PCS speaks of the sacramental meaning of those who are present for the celebration of the sacrament. "Because of its very nature as a sign, the sacrament of the anointing of the sick should be celebrated with members of the family and other representatives of the Christian community whenever this is possible. Then the sacrament is seen for what it is—a part of the prayer of the Church and an encounter with the Lord" (PCS, 99). Those gathered around the sick person are not merely bystanders or onlookers. Rather, they are signs that the sacrament is truly "the prayer of the Church and an encounter with the Lord" (PCS, 99). Whether few or many, they are signs of the Church universal and the sacramental celebration as "a meeting of God's children with their Father, in Christ and the Holy Spirit" (CCC, 1153).

---

2. Ibid.

THE GREETING

Since the Sacrament of the Anointing of the Sick is often celebrated with small groups, and not infrequently with only the priest and the sick person, it is good to remember that "liturgical services are not private functions, but are celebrations belonging to the Church, which is the 'sacrament of unity,' namely, the holy people united and ordered under their bishops" (SC, 26). One of the ways that the ecclesial reality of every sacramental celebration is effected, as we noted in chapter 1, is through the priest's greeting: "The Lord be with you," and the people's response, "And with your spirit." This greeting also begins the celebration of the Sacrament of the Anointing of the Sick and through it the body of Christ, head and members, is made present. This presence is then acknowledged in the instruction that immediately follows: "My dear friends, we are gathered here in the name of our Lord Jesus Christ who is present among us" (PCS, 117). Recall also the different ways that Christ is present: in the assembly, in the priest, in his word, and in the Eucharistic species, which is "presence in the fullest sense: that is to say, it is a substantial presence by which Christ, God and man, makes himself wholly and entirely present" (CCC, 1374). As we grow in our understanding and discernment of this sacramental presence, we can enter more fully in the exhortation that concludes the instruction: "Let us therefore commend our sick brother/sister N. to the grace and power of Christ, that he may save him/her and raise him/her up" (PCS, 117). We are commending our sick to Christ who is really, truly, sacramentally present.

LITURGY OF ANOINTING

The Liturgy of Anointing which follows includes three elements: "the prayer of faith, the laying on of hands, and the anointing with oil" (PCS, 104). We will now consider each in turn.

Prayer of Faith

Faith is central to this—and every—sacramental celebration, for "the sick person will be saved by personal faith and the faith of the Church, which looks back to the death and resurrection of Christ, the source of the sacrament's power (see James 5:15), and looks ahead to the future kingdom that is pledged in the sacraments" (PCS, 7). In the sacramental celebration "faith itself is manifested" (PCS, 7). It must be manifested "both in the minister of the sacrament and, even more importantly, in the recipient" (PCS, 7). We encounter a moving example of this personal faith in the Gospel account of the woman who had suffered from a hemorrhage for twelve years and was healed by touching the hem of Jesus' garment (Mk 5:25–34). St. Peter Chrysologus has given us a vivid, almost eyewitness account of this moment: "She who feels unworthy in body, draws near in heart to the physician. In faith she touches God. With her hand she touches his garment, knowing that both healing and forgiveness may be bestowed on this stratagem, undertaken due to the demands of modesty, and not as she otherwise would have preferred. . . . In an instant, faith cures where human skill had failed through twelve years."[3] St. Ephrem the Syrian describes the twofold witness of this healing: "If she was a witness to his divinity, he in turn was a witness to her faith. . . . He saw through to her hidden faith, and gave her a visible healing."[4] Although the faith of the minister and recipient are vital, in the sacramental celebration "the community, asking God's help for the sick, makes its prayer of faith in response to God's word and in a spirit of trust (see James 5:14–15). . . . It is the people of God who pray in faith" (PCS, 105).

Furthermore, this prayer of faith "is the epiclesis proper to this sacrament" (CCC, 1519), invoking the power and action of the Holy Spirit. "The prayer of faith," wrote St. Hilary of Arles in the fifth century, "is the consensus of the whole church, as it is said in the Gospel: 'Whatever you ask in my name shall be done for you.'"[5] Of particular importance in this regard is the Prayer after Anointing: "The prayer following [the anointing] belongs to the very heart of the sacred action, since the 'Prayer of Faith' is according to Jas 5:14f. a constituent element of the liturgy. The new Rite offers as well as this prayer a choice of other prayers which are adapted to the personal situation of recipient."[6] For example, the prayer for the terminally ill asks for support, comfort,

---

3. Thomas C. Oden and Christopher A. Hall, eds., *Mark, New Testament II*, Ancient Christian Commentary on Scripture (Downers Grove, IL: InterVarsity, 1998), 70.

4. Ibid.

5. Gerald L. Bray, *James, 1–2 Peter, 1–3 John, Jude*, New Testament XI, Ancient Christian Commentary on Scripture (Downers Grove, IL: InterVarsity, 2000), 60.

6. Michael Kunzler, *The Church's Liturgy*, trans. by Placed Murray, OSB, Henry O'Shea, OSB, Cilian Ó Sé, OSB (NY: Continuum, 2001), 289.

and "the strength to fight against evil" (PCS, 125C), and the prayer before surgery includes a petition for the Lord to grant his healing gifts to the surgeons and nurses and for the patient to respond to God's healing will and rejoin the community at God's "altar of praise" (PCS, 125E).

Laying On of Hands

Before the priest anoints the sick person, he silently imposes his hands on the head of the sick person. This gesture has several meanings. First, it indicates that the recipient is the particular focus of the Church's prayer. Second, the imposition of hands is a sign of blessing, for "we pray that by the power of God's healing grace the sick person may be restored to health or at least strengthened in time of illness" (PCS, 106). Third, it is the sign of the invocation of the Holy Spirit, as "the Church prays for the coming of the Holy Spirit upon the sick person" (PCS, 106). Finally, it is the biblical gesture of healing, "and indeed Jesus' own usual manner of healing" (PCS, 106) (see for example Mk 5:23; 6:5; 8:25; 10:16; Lk 4:40; and 13:13). "Thus, the imposition of hands, a privileged sacramental sign, derives its meaning from Christ's ministry. The healing of sickness, connected with Christ's Resurrection, is an occasion for the showing forth of God's glory; it is a special and theophanic moment (see Jn 11:4)."[7]

Anointing with Oil

Anointing with oil is a rich sign of healing. The Old Testament prophet Isaiah laments the wounds of sinful Israel that are not "eased with salve" (1:6). The Good Samaritan of Luke's Gospel dressed the wounds of his injured neighbor with oil and wine (Lk 10:34). In Mark's account of the Gospel, Christ sent the Twelve to continue his healing ministry, and they "anointed with oil many who were sick and cured them" (6:13). The Letter of James confirms that the early Church continued this healing ministry: "Is anyone among you sick? He should summon the presbyters of the church, and they should pray over him and anoint him with oil in the name of the Lord" (5:14). In his commentary on this verse, Hilary of Arles says that "the grace of mercy is symbolized by

---

7. Haffner. *The Sacramental Mystery*, 173.

oil."[8] Oil as a sign of healing is an excellent example of how the Sacred Scriptures help us understand the meaning of sacramental signs.

There are additional meanings. The *Catechism* says that anointing the sick with oil "expresses healing and comfort" (1294). *The Roman Catechism*, the catechism mandated by the Council of Trent and published in 1566, describes the fittingness of oil as a sign for this sacrament: "Oil is very efficacious in soothing bodily pain, and the power of this Sacrament lessens the pain and anguish of the soul. Oil also restores health, brings joy, feeds light, and is very efficacious in refreshing bodily fatigue. All these effects signify what the divine power accomplishes in the sick man through the administration of this Sacrament."[9] According to the PCS, anointing the sick with oil signifies not only healing but also "strengthening, and the presence of the Spirit" (PCS, 107). "The Church's use of oil for healing," concludes the PCS "is closely related to its remedial use in soothing and comforting the sick and in restoring the tired and the weak. Thus the sick person is strengthened to fight against the physically and spiritually debilitating effects of illness" (PCS, 107).

Activity

Summarize five different meanings of anointing with oil. How do these meanings reflect different aspects of the Sacrament of the Anointing of the Sick?

The prayer of blessing over the oil deepens our understanding of this sacramental sign and expresses the power of this sacramental sign.

> God of all consolation,
> you chose and sent your Son to heal the world.
> Graciously listen to our prayer of faith:
> send the power of your Holy Spirit, the Consoler,
> into this precious oil, this soothing ointment,
> this rich gift, this fruit of the earth.
> Bless this oil + and sanctify it for our use.
> Make this oil a remedy for all who are anointed with it;

---

8. Gerald Bray, ed., *James, 1–2 Peter, 1–3 John, Jude*, 60.

9. *The Catechism of the Council of Trent*, trans. John A. McHugh, OP, and Charles J. Callan, OP (Rockford, IL: Tan Books and Publishers, 1982), 309.

> heal them in body, in soul, and in spirit,
> and deliver them from every affliction. (PCS, 123)

This prayer begins by invoking the Holy Spirit upon the oil: "send the power of your Holy Spirit, the Consoler, into this precious oil, this soothing ointment, this rich gift, this fruit of the earth." This epiclesis acknowledges the oil as a rich gift and fruit of God's creation and imbues the oil with the power of the Spirit. The sign of the cross is then made over the oil: "Bless this oil + and sanctify it for our use." Finally, the prayer expresses the comprehensive healing for which the Church prays—healing in body, soul and spirit, and deliverance from every affliction. In summary, "the prayer of blessing the oil of the sick reminds us, furthermore, that the oil of anointing is the sacramental sign of the presence, power, and grace of the Holy Spirit" (PCS, 107). "The anointing of the Spirit, this mysterious oil that penetrates our mortal bodies, is like the new myrrh that the Spouse pours on the suffering members of her Lord."[10]

If the oil has already been blessed, the Thanksgiving over Blessed Oil (PCS, 40) is said. Especially notable is the prayer's Trinitarian structure. It begins by praising the Father who sent his Son "to live among us and bring us salvation." It then praises the Son who humbled himself "to share in our humanity and . . . heal our infirmities." It next praises the Holy Spirit, the Consoler, whose "unfailing power gives us strength in our bodily weakness." After each invocation, the congregation responds, "Blessed be God who heals us in Christ." The entire thanksgiving concludes by asking, "God of mercy, ease the sufferings and comfort the weakness of your servants whom the Church anoints with this holy oil" (PCS, 140). In place of this thanksgiving, the priest may give an explanation of the meaning of the blessed oil, an alternative the PCS encourages "when the sick person is in a hospital and other sick people present do not take part in the celebration of the sacrament" (PCS, 41).

In the celebration of the sacrament, the anointing is accompanied by the essential words of the sacrament, the authoritative and performative word of Christ. First the priest anoints the forehead saying, "Through this holy anointing may the Lord in his love and mercy help you with the grace of the Holy Spirit." He then anoints the hands

---

10. Corbon, *The Wellspring of Worship*, 171.

saying, "May the Lord who frees you from sin save you and raise you up." The PCS also permits additional or alternative anointings: "Depending upon the culture and traditions of the place, as well as the condition of the sick person, the priest may also anoint additional parts of the body, for example, the area of pain or injury" (PCS, 124). If he does so, however, he does not repeat the essential words. The essential words were modified following the Second Vatican Council so that, "by reflecting the words of James, [they] may better express the effects of the sacrament" (PCS, Paul VI, *Apostolic Constitution*). The petitions that the Lord would "save", "raise up," and "free from sin" are taken from James 5:15: "the prayer of faith will *save* the sick person, and the Lord will *raise him up*. If he has committed any sins, he will be *forgiven*." These petitions can be understood in a twofold sense. "The sacrament is not administered solely with regard to the future fate of a person's soul, but also with regard to his body, beset by weakness and frailty, for sickness concerns the whole person whom the Lord will help and save in the manner which is best fitting for the individual."[11] Their focus is both the present moment and eternity, this life and eternal life.

These words and actions are the essential signs of the sacrament. Their effectiveness is further enhanced by "a generous use of oil so that it will be seen and felt by the sick person as a sign of the Spirit's healing and strengthening presence. For the same reason, it is not desirable to wipe off the oil after the anointing" (PCS, 107). The simplicity of these sacramental signs belies the paschal power that they communicate. St. Thomas Aquinas offers a moving description of the appropriateness of this sacramental sign in the context of anointing the dying: "The spiritual healing, which is given at the end of life, ought to be complete, since there is no other to follow; it ought also to be gentle, lest hope, of which the dying stand in utmost need, be shattered rather than fostered. Now oil has a softening effect, it penetrates to the very heart of a thing, and spreads over it. Hence, in both the foregoing respects, it is a suitable matter for this sacrament."[12]

---

11. Kunzler, *The Church's Liturgy*, 289.
12. Monti, *A Sense of the Sacred*, 235.

Sprinkling with Holy Water

The celebration of this sacrament can include sprinkling with holy water as part of the introductory rite. Holy water is an example of a *sacramental*. Sacramentals are sacred signs instituted by the Church "which bear a resemblance to the sacraments" (CCC, 1667). The effects which they signify "are obtained through the intercession of the Church" (CCC, 1667). They differ from sacraments in three important ways.

1. The Seven Sacraments have been instituted by Christ, while sacramentals are instituted by the Church.
2. The sacraments are effective whenever they are celebrated using the rite approved by the Church by the proper minister who, in doing so, intends what the Church intends.[13] Sacramentals are effective through the prayer of the Church.
3. Sacraments confer grace whenever they are celebrated "in accordance with the intention of the Church" (CCC, 1128), while sacramentals "prepare us to receive grace and dispose us to cooperate with it" (CCC, 1670) and "sanctify different circumstances of life" (CCC, 1677).

Sacramentals usually include a prayer and a sign such as the sign of the cross or the sprinkling of holy water. Examples of sacramentals include blessings of persons, places, meals, and things, and exorcisms.

The use of holy water is an ancient tradition. Water was used in purifying sprinklings in French monasteries in the early Middle Ages. Beginning in the eighth century, this developed into a blessing of water and sprinkling before the Eucharist. It was adopted by parish churches and incorporated into the Missal of 1570. The meaning of the sprinkling changed from purification to a recalling of Baptism, as the Rite for Blessing and Sprinkling of Water in the current Missal explains: "Dear brethren, let us humbly beseech the Lord our God to bless this water he has created, which will be sprinkled on us as a memorial of our Baptism" (Appendix II).

---

13. "This is the meaning of the Church's affirmation that the sacraments act *ex opere operato* (literally: 'by the very fact of the action's being performed'), i.e., by virtue of the saving work of Christ, accomplished once for all. . . . From the moment that a sacrament is celebrated in accordance with the intention of the Church, the power of Christ and his Spirit acts in and through it, independently of the personal holiness of the minister" (CCC, 1128).

Litany

In the Rite for the Anointing outside of Mass, the Liturgy of Anointing begins with a litany. This is a form of prayer consisting of a series of petitions, said or sung, with a fixed response, such as "Lord, have mercy" or "pray for us." It is divided into two parts: a series of petitions addressed directly to God, and the invocation of a series of saints. The origins of this prayer are obscure, although there are examples from Jewish and pagan sources. The litany was used in the early Church before the dismissal of the catechumens (those preparing for Baptism), who did not participate in the prayers of the faithful. There is evidence that this litanic prayer form was used in Rome before 225.

Litanies invoking the intercession of the saints are found in a number of liturgical celebrations such as the Sacraments of Baptism, Matrimony, and Holy Orders as well as the Easter Vigil. They are also part of private devotions, such as the Litany of the Sacred Heart and the Litany of Loreto. In these celebrations they invoke the intercession of the saints and are an example of the union of the earthly Church with the heavenly Church that occurs in every liturgical celebration. The liturgy, as we noted in chapter 2, is unceasingly celebrated in heaven by Christ, our high priest, "with the holy Mother of God, the apostles, all the saints, and the multitude of those who have already entered the kingdom" (CCC, 1187). When we celebrate the liturgy, we are "entering into the liturgy of the heavens that has always been taking place. Earthly liturgy is liturgy because and only because it joins what is already in process, the greater reality."[14] We seek the intercession of the saints because they are present at our liturgical celebrations, and their intercession is efficacious.

In the PCS we find two kinds of litanies, one invoking the saints and the other petitions directed to God. The celebration of the Anointing of the Sick both within and outside Mass includes a litany addressed to God, which is the first part of the Liturgy of Anointing. This is the litany for the Anointing outside of Mass:

> Come and strengthen him/her through this holy anointing:
> Lord, have mercy.
> Free him/her from all harm: Lord, have mercy.

---

14. Joseph Ratzinger, *A New Song to the Lord: Faith in Christ and Liturgy Today*, trans. Martha M. Matesich (New York: Crossroad, 1996), 166.

> Free him/her from sin and all temptation: Lord, have mercy.
> Relieve the sufferings of all the sick [here present]: Lord, have mercy.
> Assist all those dedicated to the care of sick: Lord, have mercy.
> Give life and health to our brother/sister N., on whom we lay our hands in your name: Lord, have mercy. (PCS, 121)

This litany focuses on strengthening the sick against harm and temptation, the recovery of health, and support for those who care for the sick.

The Commendation of the Dying includes a litany invoking the intercession of the saints. It is a rite for the dying person who has been "united with Christ in his passage out of this world to the Father" through the reception of viaticum (PCS, 212). The rite particularly recommends praying the litany "when the condition of the dying person calls for the use of brief forms of prayer" (PCS, 219). It begins with the Kyrie—"Lord, have mercy. Christ, have mercy. Lord, have mercy"—followed by the invocation of particular saints, to which those present respond, "pray for him/her." In addition to the saints given in the rite, "special mention may be made of the patron saints of the dying person, of the family, and of the parish" (PCS, 219). Following the invocation of the saints, the litany petitions God's mercy: "From all evil," "From every sin," "From Satan's power," "At the moment of death," "From everlasting death," and "On the day of judgment" (PCS, 219A). The response to each of these is, "Lord, save your people." It concludes with specific petitions for the dying person: "Bring N. to eternal life, first promised to him/her in baptism"; "Raise N. on the last day, for he/she has eaten the bread of life"; "Let N. share in your glory, for he/she has shared in your suffering and death" (PCS, 219A). The litany is a beautiful example of the power of God manifested through the communion of saints.

Viaticum

The celebration of Eucharist as Viaticum, "the last sacrament of Christian life," gives a particular sign value to different elements of the rite (PCS, 175). One of the distinctive features of this rite is the renewal of baptismal promises. The faithful renew their baptismal profession on different occasions, for example, at Easter and in the celebration of the sacraments of Baptism and Confirmation, which in each case have a distinctive meaning. As part of the rite of viaticum, "at the end of earthly life, the one who is dying uses the language of his or her initial commitment . . . [as] a renewal and fulfillment of initiation into the Christian mysteries, baptism leading to the eucharist" (PCS, 179). Here it is a poignant and fervent final affirmation of one's faith in the Lord he or she is soon to meet face to face.

A second liturgical sign is the sign of peace, following the litany and preparing for communion. In earlier times this "took the form of ritual kiss [and] is mentioned in the oldest writings of the New Testament" (cf. Rom 16:16; 1 Cor 16:20; 2 Cor 13:12; 1 Th 5:26; 1 Pe 5:14). In his commentary on 2 Cor 13:12, St. John Chrysostom proposes a lovely image: "We are the temple of Christ, and when we kiss each other we are kissing the porch and entrance of the temple."[15] This peace is "the pure gift of God . . . won for us by the risen Christ present in the midst of those gathered" (IOM, 128). It embraces "total well-being, a life in harmony with God and with ourselves, with our neighbors, and with the whole of creation" (IOM, 128). This exchange "acknowledges that Christ whom we receive in the sacrament is already present in our neighbor" (IOM, 129). It is not merely an expression of good will or solidarity; "it is, rather, an opening of ourselves and our neighbors to a challenge and a gift beyond ourselves, . . . the acceptance of a challenge: a gesture expressing the belief that we are members, one with another, in the body of Christ" (IOM, 129).

For the sign of peace in the celebration of Viaticum, "the minister and all who are present embrace the dying Christian" (PCS, 180). This embrace expresses diverse feelings: "the sense of leave-taking need not be concealed or denied, but the joy of Christian hope, which is the comfort and strength of the one near death, should also be evident" (PCS, 180). These conflicting emotions—sorrow and joy—characterize the challenge signified by this sign of peace. In this rite family and friends open themselves to their dying loved one, perhaps the definitive "gift beyond ourselves" (IOM, 129).

Finally, the reception of Communion has Viaticum has a distinctive meaning, for it "is the completion and crown of the Christian life on this earth, signifying that the Christian follows the Lord to eternal glory and the banquet of the heavenly kingdom" (PCS, 175). Words proper to the celebration of viaticum—"May the Lord Jesus Christ

---

15. Gerald Bray, ed., *1–2 Corinthians*, New Testament VII, Ancient Christian Commentary on Scripture (Downers Grove, IL: InterVarsity Press, 1999), 311.

protect you and lead you to eternal life"—indicate "that the reception of the Eucharist by the dying Christian is a pledge of resurrection and food for the passage through death" (PCS, 181). Reception of both the Body and Blood of Christ expresses "more fully and clearly the nature of the eucharist as a meal, one which prepares all who take part in it for the heavenly banquet" (PCS, 181).[16] The Church highly recommends the reception of Viaticum within Mass. "In this way he or she shares fully, during the final moments of this life, in the eucharistic sacrifice, which proclaims the Lord's own passing through death to life" (PCS, 177).

The depth of meaning which these signs express in the context of Viaticum explain why the Church urges that the rite be "celebrated while the dying person is still able to take part and respond" (PCS, 178). These examples—the renewal of baptismal promises, the sign of peace, and the reception of communion—reveal how familiar sacramental signs can take on new meanings in the context of the specific liturgical celebration.

CONCLUSION

The sacramental signs that comprise the Anointing of the Sick make present the healing and saving power of Christ's Paschal Mystery. The priest, together with the sick person and those present for the celebration of the sacrament together signify and make present the whole Body of Christ, head and members, both the suffering Body of Christ and the resurrected and glorified Body of Christ. Christ's performative word, which is spoken by the priest, instructs and accomplishes what it signifies (CCC, 1155). Through the litany of the saints the Church in heaven is invoked and aids the Church on earth. The Spirit acts through the imposition of hands and anointing with blessed oil to bring healing and comfort. Other signs such as the sign of the cross and the use of holy water further signify the power and action of the Spirit in

---

16. "The sick who are unable to receive under the form of bread may receive under the form of wine alone" (PCS, 181).

communicating Christ's healing power. Through these sacramental signs God the Father continues to care for his children, touching, healing, and comforting them through the power of Christ's Paschal Mystery communicated by the Holy Spirit. Those who receive this sacrament will thus find "a new sign of hope" and "a true sign of comfort and support in time of trial" (PCS, 52).

Chapter 9

Anointing of the Sick: Living the Sacrament

The Sacrament of the Anointing of the Sick "gives the grace of the Holy Spirit to those who are sick" by which "the whole person is helped and saved" (PCS, 6). The grace and gifts of this sacrament are multiple in part because they are given by the Holy Spirit who is the gift that contains all gifts (CCC, 1082). But they are also multiple because the effects of sickness are diverse. Against the weakness and anxiety that can follow upon serious illness, the Spirit imparts strength and peace. God desires the salvation of all (1 Tim 2:4; CCC, 74 and 851), so physical healing may be granted if it will benefit the person's salvation. Against the crippling consequences of unconfessed sin, the Spirit grants forgiveness and reconciliation. Against the temptation to feel abandoned by God, the Spirit imparts the grace to unite one's personal suffering to the passion of Christ. Finally, the celebration of Viaticum prepares the Christian for "passing over to eternal life" (CCC, 1532). Every gift that is needed for the help and salvation of the sick person is imparted by the Holy Spirit.

STRENGTH, PEACE, AND COURAGE

We do not possess within ourselves the resources "to overcome the difficulties that go with the condition of serious illness or the frailty of old age" (CCC, 1520). Frailty and illness test us in many ways—physically, spiritually, and emotionally. We are vulnerable to the temptations of the evil one (PCS, 6). Faith, hope, and love are all challenged. We can feel alienated and cut off from family, friends, our parish, even God. At such times we need the strength of the Lord, the peace promised by Christ (Jn 14:27), and his assurance, "Do not be afraid" (Lk 5:10). The celebration of the sacrament confers "a particular gift of the Holy Spirit, . . . one of strengthening, peace and courage" (CCC, 1520).

The prayers in the PCS include numerous petitions for strength and comfort:

> through this holy anointing
> grant N. comfort in his/her suffering.
> When he/she is afraid, give him/her courage,
> when afflicted, give him/her patience,
> when dejected, afford him/her hope,
> and when alone, assure him/her of the support of
> your holy people. (PCS, 125A)

This petition acknowledges the fear, affliction, dejection, and isolation that accompany sickness and expresses faith in the power and mercy of God to grant courage, patience, hope, and assurance of their place in the Body of Christ. The Spirit also strengthens the sick against the attacks of the evil one. One of the prayers after the anointing asks God to give the sick person "the strength to fight against evil" (PCS, 125C). The concluding blessing includes petitions for consolation, hope, and peace:

> May the God of all consolation
> bless you in every way
> and grant you hope all the days of your life. . . .
> May God fill your heart with peace
> and lead you to eternal life. (PCS, 147A)

With faith we ask the Lord: "Transform our weakness by the strength of your grace and confirm us in your covenant so that we may grow in faith and love" (PCS, 136B).

The prayers for peace and strength are sensitively adapted to those receiving the sacrament. The maternal care of God is expressed in the prayer for a child:

> Caress him/her,
> shelter him/her,
> and keep him/her in your tender care. (PCS, 125F)

The prayer for a young person acknowledges the exuberance of youth:

> Restore him/her to health and strength,
> make him/her joyful in spirit,
> and ready to embrace your will. (PCS, 125G)

The petition for the aged acknowledges their physical and spiritual needs:

> Look kindly on your servant
> who has grown weak under the burden of years.
> In this holy anointing
> he/she asks for healing in body and soul.
> Fill him/her with the strength of your Holy Spirit.
> Keep him/her firm in faith and serene in hope,
> so that he/she may give us all an example of patience
> and joyfully witness to the power of your love. (PCS, 125D)

Though frail in health, they strengthen the Body of Christ by their patient and joyful witness. The compassion, kindness, and gentleness of the Lord is given eloquent voice in these prayers for the sick of every age and condition.

RESTORED TO HEALTH

Physical healing and the return to health "if beneficial to salvation" is another effect of this sacrament (PCS, 6). Christ came among us as a man to heal and to save us, and so we confidently ask him to restore the sick to health:

> Lord Jesus Christ,
> you chose to share our human nature,
> to redeem all people, and to heal the sick.
> Look with compassion on your servant N.,
> whom we have anointed in your name with this holy oil
> for the healing of his/her body and spirit. (PCS, 125C)

This too is a grace of the Holy Spirit:

> Lord Jesus Christ, our Redeemer,
> by the grace of the Holy Spirit
> cure the weakness of your servant N.
> Heal his/her sickness . . . ;
> mercifully restore him/her to full health,
> and enable him/her to resume his/her former duties,
> for you are Lord for ever and ever. (PCS, 125B)

Christ heals in miraculous ways, but also through the skill and knowledge of doctors and nurses. A prayer for those being anointed before surgery asks

> that through the skills of surgeons and nurses
> your healing gifts may be granted to N.
> May your servant respond to your healing will
> and be reunited with us at your altar of praise. (PCS, 125E)

These petitions express the Church's faith in the present-day ministry of Christ the divine physician.

The prayers and texts for the celebration of the sacrament within Mass include frequent petitions for healing. The opening prayer for this Mass invokes God as the "eternal health of believers":

> Almighty ever-living God, eternal health of believers,
> hear our prayers for your servants who are sick:
> grant them, we implore you, your merciful help,
> so that, with their help restored,
> they may give you thanks in the midst of your Church.
> (RM, Masses and Prayers for Various Needs and Occasions, 45:
> For the Sick, Collect)

The celebration of the sacrament follows the homily and begins with the reception of the sick:

> Christ is always present when
> we gather in his name; today we welcome him
> especially as physician and healer. We pray that the
> sick may be restored to health by the gift of his mercy
> and made whole in his fullness. (PCS, 135A)

In its solicitude for the sick, the congregation is fulfilling the words of Christ who

> taught his disciples to be a community of love.
> In praying together, in sharing all things, and in caring
> for the sick, they recalled his words: "Insofar as you
> did this to one of these, you did it to me." We gather
> today to witness to this teaching and to pray in the
> name of Jesus the healer that the sick may be restored
> to health. Through this eucharist and anointing we
> invoke his healing power. (PCS, 135B)

These prayers both express and strengthen the faith of the sick and of the assembly.

Following the rite of anointing, the Mass continues with the Liturgy of the Eucharist. The Prayer over the Gifts again petitions God for healing:

> . . . receive the prayers and sacrificial offerings
> by which we implore your mercy
> for our brothers and sisters who are ill,
> that, having been anxious for them in their danger,
> we may rejoice at their recovery of health.
> (RM, Masses and Prayers for Various Needs and Occasions, 45:
> For the Sick, Prayer over the Gifts)

Another option implores healing for all of those present, and indeed for all of the faithful, since every celebration of the Mass makes present Christ's saving sacrifice for the whole world:

> In his name
> heal the ills which afflict us
> and restore to us the joy of life renewed. (PCS, 144B)

Specific petitions for the sick are provided for the Eucharistic Prayer:

> Hear especially the prayers of those who ask for healing
> in the name of your Son,
> that they may never cease to praise you
> for the wonders of your power. (PCS, 145)

After receiving the Body and Blood of the Lord, God's mercy is again invoked:

> O God, only support of our human weakness,
> show the power of your protection
> over your servants who are sick,
> that, sustained by your merciful help,
> they may be restored to your holy Church in good health.
> (RM, Masses and Prayers for Various Needs and Occasions, 45:
> For the Sick, Prayer after Communion)

The celebration of the sacrament within Mass may conclude with a threefold solemn blessing. In this blessing God is invoked as "the God of all consolation," a reference to 2 Cor 1:3–4: "Blessed be the God and Father of our Lord Jesus Christ, the Father of compassion and God all encouragement, who encourages us in our every affliction, so that we may be able to encourage those who are in any affliction with the encouragement with which we ourselves are encouraged by God." God's blessing is invoked not only for physical healing, but also for hope, salvation, peace, and eternal life.

> May the God of all consolation
> bless you in every way
> and grant you hope all the days of your life.
> May God restore you to health
> and grant you salvation.
> May God fill your heart with peace
> and lead you to eternal life. (PCS, 147A)

A second option is similar:

> May the Lord be with you to protect you.
> May he guide you and give you strength.
> May he watch over you, keep you in his care,
> and bless you with his peace. (PCS, 147B)

A third option found in *The Roman Missal* is distinctive for its explicitly Trinitarian structure:

> May God the Father bless you.
> May the Son of God heal you.
> May the Holy Spirit shed light on you.
> May God guard your body and save your soul.
> May he enlighten your heart and lead you to life on high.
> (RM, Ritual Masses, For the Conferral of the
> Anointing of the Sick)

At every stage of life, the grace and power of the Trinity are offered to draw us more deeply into the mystery of God who is love (1 Jn 4:16).

FORGIVENESS OF SINS

The forgiveness of sins is another grace of this sacrament. "If necessary, the sacrament also provides the sick person with the forgiveness of sins and the completion of Christian penance" (PCS, 6). The *Catechism* amplifies the qualifier "if necessary," explaining that the sacrament provides "the forgiveness of sins, if the sick person was not able to obtain it through the sacrament of Penance" (1532). If the sick person is conscious, he or she should be offered the Sacrament of Penance since that is the ordinary way that sins are remitted. "However, if he is unconscious, Anointing will eradicate mortal sins. A necessary condition for the forgiveness of sins is that the sinner has turned away from sin at least by a habitually continuing imperfect contrition. By Anointing of the Sick, venial sins and also temporal punishments due to sin are remitted."[1] The PCS offers the following instruction concerning those who are unconscious: "The sacrament of anointing is to be conferred on sick people who, although they have lost consciousness or the use of reason, have, as Christian believers, at least implicitly asked for it when they were in control of their faculties" (PCS, 14). If there is doubt about whether or not the recipient has died, "the priest . . . should confer the sacrament" (PCS, 15). The Church is always solicitous for the good of the whole person.

The priest may also "give the apostolic pardon for the dying" (PCS, 243 and 265). This is an example of a plenary indulgence. The PCS provides two formulas:

> By the authority which the Apostolic See has given me,
> I grant you a full pardon and the remission of all your sins
> in the name of the Father, and of the Son, + and of the Holy
> Spirit. (PCS, 201B)

and

> Through the holy mysteries of our redemption,
> may almighty God release you from all punishments
> in this life and in the life to come.
> May he open to you the gates of paradise
> and welcome you to everlasting joy. (PCS, 201A)

This is particularly encouraged by the *Manual of Indulgences* (MI), which says that when a priest administers the sacraments to those in danger of death, he "should not fail to impart the apostolic blessing to which a *plenary indulgence* is attached" (MI, 12.1; italics original).

Nevertheless, those who at the point of death cannot be attended by a priest are not denied access to the Church's treasury of "the infinite and inexhaustible value" of the salvation gained for us by Christ. "If a priest is unavailable [at the point of death], Holy Mother Church

---

1. Haffner, *The Sacramental Mystery*, 189.

benevolently grants to the Christian faithful, who are duly disposed, a plenary indulgence to be acquired at the point of death, provided they have been in the habit of reciting some prayers during their lifetime; in such a case, the Church supplies for the three conditions[2] ordinarily required for a plenary indulgence" (MI, 54). In such cases, the use of a cross or crucifix "is commendable" (MI, 54). Pastors and catechists are encouraged to ensure that the faithful "are duly made aware and frequently reminded of this salutary benefaction of the Church" (MI, 55). Again we see the Church's solicitude for the dying amidst the exigencies of life. In every circumstance she desires to strengthen them "against anxiety over death" (PCS, 6).

UNION WITH THE PASSION OF CHRIST

The grace of this sacrament also enables the sick "to associate themselves willingly with the passion and death of Christ" (PCS, 5). This is described in a number of New Testament passages cited by the PCS. In his Letter to the Romans, the Apostle Paul explained that "we are children of God, and if children, then heirs, heirs of God and joint heirs with Christ, if only we suffer with him so that we may also be glorified with him" (Rom 8:17). The Second Letter to Timothy includes this "trustworthy" saying: "If we have died with him we shall also live with him; if we persevere we shall also reign with him" (2 Tim 2:11–12). And the First Letter of Peter encourages believers to "rejoice to the extent that you share in the sufferings of Christ" (1 Pet 4:13). It was clearly the experience and understanding of the early Christians that they were not only saved by the sufferings of Christ but were also called to share in them.

But perhaps the most compelling New Testament passage is Colossians 1:24: "Now I rejoice in my sufferings for your sake, and in my flesh I am filling up what is lacking in the afflictions of Christ on behalf of his body, which is the church." Biblical scholars and theologians agree that the apostle is not implying any insufficiency in Christ's atoning work: "although variously interpreted, this phrase does not imply that Christ's atoning death on the cross was defective";[3] "Paul is not claiming to add anything to the redemptive value of the cross (to

---

2. The three conditions are sacramental confession, Eucharistic Communion, and prayer for the intention of the Pope (MI, n20, 1).

3. *New American Bible*, 310n on 1:24.

which in any case nothing is lacking)."[4] Rather, these "are the sufferings predicted for the messianic era, Matthew 24:8f.; Acts 14:22; 1 Timothy 4:1a, and are all part of the way in which God had always intended the Church to develop."[5]

St. John Paul II presented a profound reflection of this verse in his apostolic letter, *On the Christian Meaning of Human Suffering (Salvifici Doloris,* henceforth SD). Christ, through his suffering, Death, and Resurrection—the Paschal Mystery—initiated *"the union with man in the community of the Church"* (SD, 24; italics original). The Church "is continually being built up spiritually as the Body of Christ" through Baptism and the Eucharist (SD, 24). This body is the way that Christ unites himself to each Christian, because "Christ wishes to be united with every individual, and in a special way he is united with those who suffer" (SD, 24). Colossians 1:24, the saint says, is a "witness to the exceptional nature of this union" (SD, 24). Even more, it "highlights the truth *concerning the creative character of suffering"* (SD, 24; italics original).

What does he mean by "the creative character of suffering"? In what way is suffering "creative"? This is how St. John Paul II explains it. He begins by affirming the completeness of Christ's redemptive work: "The sufferings of Christ created the good of the world's redemption. This good in itself is inexhaustible and infinite. No man can add anything to it" (SD, 24). Christ achieved a complete redemption. But at this point St. John Paul II makes a careful and decisive distinction: Christ's redemption is *complete* but not *closed.*

> Christ achieved the Redemption completely and to the very limits but at the same time he did not bring it to a close. In this redemptive suffering, through which the Redemption of the world was accomplished, Christ opened himself from the beginning to every human suffering and constantly does so. (SD, 24)

Although this redemption was completely achieved at a precise moment in time, it also "lives on and in its own special way develops in the history of man" (SD, 24). St. John Paul II goes so far as to assert that an intrinsic aspect of Christ's redemptive suffering is its openness to the suffering of his disciples: "Yes, it seems to be part *of the very essence of Christ's redemptive suffering* that this suffering requires to be unceasingly completed" (SD, 24).

---

4. *New Jerusalem Bible,* 1947n.

5. Ibid.

This ongoing "openness" of Christ's redemption is part of the mystery of divine love, of God who is love (1 Jn 4:16). Christ's redemptive work, which was "accomplished through satisfactory love, *remains always open to all love* expressed in *human suffering*" (SD, 24). God's love always expresses itself in giving—"For God so loved the world that he gave his only Son" (Jn 3:16); "Christ loved the church and handed himself over for her" (Eph 5:25)—and this same love "has been poured out into our hearts through the holy Spirit that has been given to us" (Rom 5:5). "In this dimension—the dimension of love—the Redemption which has already been completely accomplished is, in a certain sense, constantly being accomplished" (SD, 24). The openness of Christ's redemptive suffering exists and is continuously accomplished only in this "dimension of love." Human suffering is a participation in Christ's self-giving love on the Cross, the definitive sign and revelation of God's love, a love rooted in the Trinity, a community of persons characterized by a mutual and eternal giving and receiving in love. "All love," writes Pope Francis, "is meant to share in the complete self-gift of the Son of God for our sake."[6]

In addition, when the sick unite their sufferings to those of Christ, they do not do so as isolated individuals, but as members of the body of Christ, his Church, through the gift of the Spirit. "By communicating his Spirit, Christ mystically constitutes as his body those brothers of his who are called together from every nation" (CCC, 788). The Church is not only "gathered *around him*; she is united *in him*, in his body" (CCC, 789). This unity in Christ means that Christians are also "linked to one another, especially to those who are suffering, to the poor and persecuted" (CCC, 806). For this reason, Christ's redemptive work "lives and develops as the body of Christ, the Church, and in this dimension every human suffering, by reason of the loving union with Christ, completes the suffering of Christ" (SD, 24). The Church is "the space or context in which human sufferings complete the sufferings of Christ. Only within this radius and dimension of the Church as the Body of Christ, which continually develops in space and time, can one think and speak of 'what is lacking' in the sufferings of Christ. The Apostle, in fact, makes this clear when he writes of 'completing what is lacking in Christ's afflictions for the sake of his body, that is, the Church'"(SD, 24). Only within the space-context-radius-dimension of the mystical Body of

---

6. Francis, *Lumen Fidei, The Light of Faith* (Washington, DC: USCCB, 2013), 32.

Christ can we unite our sufferings with Christ, for the Church is "the fullness of the one who fills all things in every way" (Eph 1:23).

The mystery of this union of our sufferings with Christ is beautifully summarized in the Prayer over the Gifts for the celebration of the sacrament within Mass: "as these simple gifts of bread and wine will be transformed into the risen Lord, so may he unite our sufferings with his and cause us to rise to new life" (PCS, 144). Uniting of our sufferings with Christ involves a transformation that is analogous to the transformation of the bread and wine into the Body and Blood of Christ. And in this transformation is found the promise and hope of new life.

FOR THE GOOD OF THE PEOPLE OF GOD

This union with the sufferings of Christ brings about an interior transformation that overcomes *"the sense of the uselessness of suffering"* (SD, 27; italics original) and reveals how personal sufferings "contribute to the good of the People of God" (CCC, 1522). A feeling of uselessness, writes St. John Paul II, "is sometimes very strongly rooted in human suffering. This feeling not only consumes the person interiorly, but seems to make him a burden to others. The person feels condemned to receive help and assistance from others, and at the same time seems useless to himself" (SD, 27). The union of suffering "brings with it the interior certainty that the suffering person 'completes what is lacking in Christ's afflictions' (Col 1:24); the certainty that in the spiritual dimension of the work of Redemption *he is serving,* like Christ, *the salvation of his brothers and sisters.* Therefore he is carrying out an irreplaceable service" (SD, 27).

This service of salvation stems from the purifying nature of suffering "which clears the way for the grace which transforms human souls" (SD, 27). As sharers in the sufferings of Christ, the sick "preserve in their own sufferings a very special *particle of the infinite treasure* of the world's Redemption, and can share this treasure with others" (SD, 27). In this way, "suffering, more than anything else, makes present in the history of humanity the powers of the Redemption. In that 'cosmic' struggle between the spiritual powers of good and evil, spoken of in the Letter to the Ephesians (6:12), human sufferings, united to the redemptive suffering of Christ, *constitute a special support for the powers of good,* and open the way to the victory of these salvific powers" (SD, 27). St. John

Paul II summarizes "this strange paradox" in a vivid image: "the springs of divine power gush forth precisely in the midst of human weakness" (SD, 27).

In the opening prayer for the Mass for the Sick we pray for this union, asking that God would "grant that all who are oppressed by pain, distress or other afflictions may know that they are chosen among those proclaimed blessed and are united to Christ in his suffering for the salvation of the world" (RM, Masses and Prayers for Various Needs and Occasions, 45: For the Sick, Collect). "The Anointing of the Sick, for its part, unites the sick with Christ's self-offering for the salvation of all, so that they too, within the mystery of the communion of saints, can participate in the redemption of the world" (SacCar, 22). The suffering of Christ's members reveals a specific salvific dimension of the communion of saints.

THE SACRAMENT OF THE DEPARTING

Just as the sick unite their sufferings to the Passion of Christ, so those who at the end of their earthly life unite their death to the death of Jesus. They view "it as a step towards him and an entrance into everlasting life" (CCC, 1020). While the Sacrament of the Anointing of the Sick is for those who suffer from serious illness or infirmity, "even more rightly is it given to those at the point of departing this life; so it is also called *sacramentum exeuntium* (the sacrament of those departing)" (CCC, 1523). It is the source of multiple graces. First, it "completes our conformity to the death and Resurrection of Christ, just as Baptism began it" (CCC, 1523). It also "completes the holy anointings that mark the whole Christian life: that of Baptism which sealed the new life in us, and that of Confirmation which strengthened us for the combat of this life" (CCC, 1523). Finally, it "fortifies the end of our earthly life like a solid rampart for the final struggles before entering the Father's house" (CCC, 1523).

While circumstances often make it necessary to celebrate the Anointing of the Sick and Viaticum at the very end of life, the meaning and grace of these two sacraments is more clearly brought out when the Anointing of the Sick is "celebrated at the beginning of a serious illness. Viaticum, celebrated when death is close, will then be better understood as the last sacrament of Christian life" (PCS, 175). For the dying, receiving the Body and Blood of the Lord "has a particular significance and importance. It is the seed of eternal life and the power of resurrection, according to the words of the Lord: 'He who eats my flesh and drinks my blood has eternal life, and I will raise him up at the last day' (Jn 6:54). The sacrament of Christ once dead and now risen, the Eucharist is here the sacrament of passing over from death to life, from this world to the Father" (CCC, 1524).

The texts from the celebration of Viaticum express the meaning and effect of this final sacrament of the Christian. The rite offers two formulas to accompany the showing of the Body of Christ: "Jesus Christ is the food for our journey; he calls us to the heavenly table" (PCS, 207A); "This is the bread of life. Taste and see that the Lord is good" (PCS, 207B). The first formula recalls the meaning of *viaticum* as provision for the journey to the Father and his invitation to the eschatological banquet. In his prayer of thanksgiving after Mass, St. Thomas Aquinas describes the "heavenly table" as "that banquet beyond all telling, where with your Son and the Holy Spirit you are the true light of your Saints, fullness of satisfied desire, eternal gladness, consummate delight and perfect happiness" (RM, Appendix, Thanksgiving after Mass). The second formula is drawn from two scriptural texts, the words of Jesus in John 6:48, "I am the bread of life," and a verse from Psalm 34, "Taste and see that the LORD is good" (v. 9). Commenting on this verse, Arnobius the Younger wrote, "Taste the body of life and see how sweet is the Lord. He has life in himself who eats his flesh and drinks his blood, and then he will be blessed."[7] This psalm, either whole or just verse 9 or verse 6 ("Look to him and be radiant, and your faces may not blush for shame"), was part of the Mass as "a Communion song almost everywhere in ancient Christendom."[8]

The texts for communion also speak of our final healing and entrance into the Lord's presence. After the showing of the host, either immediately before or after the recipient says "Amen," the minister says, "May the Lord Jesus Christ protect you and lead you to eternal life" (PCS, 193). The prayers after communion continue these themes.

---

7. Craig A. Blaising and Carmen S. Hardin, eds., *Psalms 1–50*, Ancient Christian Commentary on Scripture, Old Testament, vol. 7 (Downers Grove, IL: InterVarsity Press, 2008), 262.

8. Joseph A. Jungmann, *The Mass of the Roman Rite: Its Origins and Development*, vol. 2 (Vienna, Austria: Herder Verlag, 1949), 392.

In this Eucharist God has refreshed his servant with heavenly food and drink, the Body and Blood of Christ that offer "eternal healing" (PCS, 209A) and "a lasting remedy for body and soul" (PCS, 209B). God is asked to lead the dying "safely into the kingdom of light" (PCS, 209A) and that, "refreshed . . . with the body and blood of your Son," the dying may enter his "kingdom in peace" (PCS, 209C). In the Eucharist as viaticum the dying receive him, the bread of heaven, the one who promises to protect them and lead them to eternal life.

The Sacraments of Penance and Anointing and Viaticum prepare the dying for their final journey.

> When the Church for the last time speaks Christ's words of pardon and absolution over the dying Christian, seals him for the last time with a strengthening anointing, and gives him Christ in viaticum as nourishment for the journey, she speaks with gentle assurance:

> > Go forth, Christian soul, from this world
> > in the name of God the almighty Father,
> > who created you,
> > in the name of Jesus Christ, the Son of the living God,
> > who suffered for you,
> > in the name of the Holy Spirit,
> > who was poured out upon you.
> > Go forth, faithful Christian!
> > May you live in peace this day,
> > may your home be with God in Zion,
> > with Mary, the virgin Mother of God,
> > with Joseph, and all the angels and saints. . . .
> > May you return to [your Creator]
> > who formed you from the dust of the earth.
> > May holy Mary, the angels, and all the saints
> > come to meet you as you go forth from this life. . . .
> > May you see your Redeemer face to face. (CCC, 1020,
> > quoting PCS, 220)

This prayer of commendation for the dying is spiritually and theologically rich. It beautifully expresses salvation as a work of the Trinity, the communion of saints, and death as a saving and loving encounter with Christ "face to face." Just as the sacraments of Baptism, Confirmation, and Eucharist complete our initiation into Christ and his Church, "so too it can be said that Penance, the Anointing of the Sick and the Eucharist as viaticum constitute at the end of Christian life 'the sacraments that prepare for our heavenly homeland' or the sacraments that complete the earthly pilgrimage" (CCC, 1525).

CONCLUSION

The graces conferred by the Anointing of the Sick reflect the tenderness and compassion of God, who "knows how we are formed, remembers that we are dust" (Ps 103:14). In this sacrament "the Spirit configures us to Jesus in his sufferings, transforms our weakness into life-giving love, and completes in our members the irresistible passage of him who is head of the body. Then that which Ezekiel glimpsed in his vision of the dry bones (Ezek 37:1–14) becomes a reality for us; the Spirit of life lays hold of us in our weakness, and the 'seal of his gift' becomes a pledge of resurrection that nothing can take from us."[9] The words of the Preface for the Mass for the Sick are a fitting conclusion to the transformation wrought by this sacrament: "Through your gift of the Spirit, you bless us, even now, with comfort and healing, strength and hope, forgiveness and peace" (PCS, 145).

Sacraments of Healing

You are preparing to visit someone who has just been diagnosed with cancer. Your parish priest will be coming tomorrow to celebrate the Sacrament of the Anointing of the Sick. He has asked you to prepare him/her for the reception of the sacrament. Explain how the sacrament confers each of the following:

1. Comfort
2. Healing (temporal/eternal)
3. Strength
4. Hope
5. Forgiveness
6. Peace

---

9. Jean Corbon, *The Wellspring of Worship*, 2nd ed., trans. Matthew J. O'Connell (San Francisco: Ignatius, 2005), 171.

Chapter 10

The Sacraments of Healing: Conclusion

Through the sacraments of Christian initiation—Baptism, Confirmation, and Eucharist—we receive the new life of Christ. But "we carry this life 'in earthen vessels' (2 Cor 4:7), and . . . we are still in our 'earthly tent' (2 Cor 5:1), subject to suffering, illness, and death" and can by sinning weaken or even lose this new life (CCC, 1420). The Lord Jesus Christ, "physician of our bodies and souls," who during his earthly ministry forgave sinners and healed the sick, "has willed that his Church continue, in the power of the Holy Spirit, his work of healing and salvation, even among her own members" (CCC, 1421). She does so through the sacraments of healing, Penance and the Anointing of the Sick.

The close relationship between these two sacraments of healing is especially evident in Jesus' healing of the paralytic in Mark 2:1–12. Pope Emeritus Benedict XVI and the Church fathers offer illuminating interpretations of this event. Pope Emeritus Benedict XVI considers this scene "to be of key significance for the question of Jesus' mission."[1] Jesus is at home, teaching a large crowd gathered in and around the house. Four men carrying a paralytic try to get near Jesus but cannot because of the crowd, so they open the roof and lower the paralytic on a mat. "The sick man's very existence was a plea," writes Pope Emeritus Benedict XVI, "an urgent appeal for salvation, to which Jesus responded in a way that was quite contrary to the expectation of the bearers and of the sick man himself."[2] Seeing their faith, Jesus says to the paralytic, "Child, your sins are forgiven" (2:5). "This was the last thing anyone was expecting. This was the last thing they were concerned about. The paralytic needed to be able to walk, not to be delivered from his sins. The scribes criticized the theological presumption of Jesus' words: the

---

1. Joseph Ratzinger (Pope Benedict XVI), *Jesus of Nazareth: The Infancy Narratives*, trans. Philip J. Whitemore (NY: Image, 2012), 44.

2. Ibid., 43–44.

sick man and those around him were disappointed, because Jesus had apparently overlooked the man's real need."[3]

Jesus immediately discerns the thoughts of those present and says to them, "Why are you thinking such things in your hearts? Which is easier, to say to the paralytic, 'Your sins are forgiven,' or to say, 'Rise, pick up your mat and walk?'" (2:8–9). Then, to demonstrate his authority to forgive sins, he says to the paralytic, "I say to you, rise, pick up your mat, and go home" (2:11). The Church fathers see in this scene the Lord's comprehensive care of us. Clement of Alexandria writes, "The good Instructor, Wisdom, who is the Word of the Father who assumed human flesh, cares for the whole nature of his creature. The all-sufficient Physician of humanity, the Savior, heals both body and soul conjointly."[4] Hilary of Poitiers interprets this as a sign that Jesus is leading sinners back to paradise: "First he granted remission of sins; next he showed his ability to restore health. Then, with the taking up of the pallet, he made it clear that bodies would be free from infirmity and suffering; lastly, with the paralytic's return to his home, he showed that believers are being given back the way to paradise from which Adam, the parent of all, who became profligate from the stain of sin, had proceeded."[5] This miracle is a beautiful compendium of the whole history of salvation.

Common to both sacraments, according to Jean Corbon, is "the need of overcoming death in its root, which is sin."[6] Our divinization (2 Pt 1:4), or conformity to Christ, he continues, "can come to pass only through the gradual elimination of the movement of rebellion by which our wounded hearts are wrung."[7] The two sacraments of healing give us "a participation in the saving love of their Lord, who here and now takes upon himself their wounds of nature and of will."[8] Furthermore, the frequency with which we receive these sacraments is not predetermined. Instead, "it depends on the course of the divine

---

3. Ibid., 44.

4. Thomas C. Oden and Christopher A. Hall, eds., *Mark*, Ancient Christian Commentary on Scripture, New Testament II (Downers Grove, IL: InterVaristy Press, 1998), 26–27.

5. Manlio Simonetti, ed., *Matthew 1–13*, Ancient Christian Commentary on Scripture, New Testament Ia (Downers Grove, IL: InterVarsity Press, 2001), 175.

6. Corbon, *The Wellspring of Worship*, 172.

7. Ibid.

8. Ibid.

health—sanctification—which Christians freely accept by joining their wills to the energy of the Holy Spirit."[9]

The account of the healing of the paralytic concludes with a description of the crowd's reaction to what they have just seen. "They were all astounded and glorified God, saying, 'We have never seen anything like this'" (Mk 2:12). Having witnessed the miracle of forgiveness and healing, the crowd disperses in awe and praise. This concluding verse is the inspiration for one of the dismissal formulas of the Mass: "Go in peace, glorifying the Lord by your life" (RM, Order of Mass, 144). It is, I think, a fitting response to the sacraments of healing, for through them Christ touches us with his healing love and draws us to himself. May we too continually praise him, acknowledge that we have never seen anything like his gracious healing, and glorify him by our lives.

---

9. Ibid.

FURTHER READING

Primary Sources: Collections

Benedict XVI. *Sacrament of Charity* (*Sacramentum Caritatis*). Boston: Pauline, 2007.
    A rich and comprehensive discussion of the Sacrament of the Eucharist.
It is divided into three main sections: "The Eucharist, A Mystery to be
Believed"; "The Eucharist, A Mystery to be Celebrated"; and "The Eucharist,
A Mystery to be Lived." Also discusses the relationship of the Eucharist to
each of the other sacraments and the Trinitarian dimension of the Eucharist.

———. *Verbum Domini* (*The Word of the Lord*). Boston: Pauline, 2010.
    This excellent presentation of the Word of God is divided into three
sections: "The God Who Speaks"; "The Word of God and the Church"; and
"The Church's Mission: To Proclaim the Word of God to the World." Of
particular interest for this book is the section entitled "The Liturgy: Privileged
Setting for the Word of God."

Bishops' Committee on the Liturgy. *Introduction to the Order of Mass*. Pastoral
Liturgy Series, vol.1. Washington, DC: United States Conference of Catholic
Bishops, 2003.
    This resource is a good introduction to the Eucharist. Especially relevant
to this book is the section entitled "The Eucharistic Celebration and Its
Symbols." It is a useful resource for all catechists.

Flannery, Austin, OP, ed. *Vatican Council II: The Basic Sixteen Documents*.
New ed. Collegeville, MN: Liturgical Press, 2014.
    This is the classic collection of the sixteen major documents of the
Second Vatican Council.

John Paul II. *On the Christian Meaning of Human Suffering*. Boston: Pauline, 1984.
    In his apostolic letter, St. John Paul II offers insights into the mystery and
meaning of human suffering based on key biblical passages such as the book
of Job, Isaiah 53, the Passion of Christ, and the parable of the Good
Samaritan.

———. *Reconciliation and Penance*. Boston: Pauline, 1984.
    St. John Paul II discusses the mystery of sin and forgiveness under
three headings: "Conversion and Reconciliation: the Church's Task and
Commitment"; "The Love That Is Greater Than Sin"; and "The Pastoral
Ministry of Penance and Reconciliation." As always, he offers profound
theological and pastoral insights.

Secondary Sources

Carstens, Christopher, and Douglas Martis. *Mystical Body Mystical Voice: Encountering Christ in the Words of the Mass*. Chicago: Liturgy Training Publications, 2011.

In addition to being an excellent resource on the Mass, part 1 is an excellent, easy-to-read overview of sacramental theology.

Corbon, Jean. *The Wellspring of Worship*. Translated by Matthew J. O'Connell. 2nd ed. San Francisco: Ignatius, 2005.

This is a classic study of the liturgy by one of the principal authors of the section on prayer in the *Catechism of the Catholic Church*. Corbon's emphasis on the role of the Holy Spirit in the liturgy is particularly illuminating.

Dallen, James. *The Reconciling Community: The Rite of Penance*. Studies in the Reformed Rites of the Catholic Church, vol. 3. Collegeville, MN: The Liturgical Press, 1991.

Dallen presents a thorough treatment of the history of the Sacrament of Penance, its reform after the Second Vatican Council, and a theological and practical discussion of the current rite.

Daniélou, Jean, SJ. *The Bible and the Liturgy*. Notre Dame, IN: Notre Dame University Press, 1956.

This is an analysis of the liturgical language of the sacraments of Baptism, Confirmation, and the Eucharist as well as the Sabbath as explained by the Fathers of the Church based on the Sacred Scriptures and Sacred Tradition. This is an excellent resource for those interested in further study of mystagogical catechesis.

Haffner, Paul. *The Sacramental Mystery*. Herefordshire: Gracewing, 2007. (Available in the US from LTP.)

This is one of the best introductions to sacramental theology—concise, clear, and thorough. It is an excellent reference for all catechists.

Kasza, John C. *Understanding Sacramental Healing: Anointing and Viaticum*. Chicago: Hillenbrand Books, 2007.

Kasza offers a concise history of the sacrament, a discussion of its reform after the Second Vatican Council, and an analysis of its celebration. Particularly helpful is his discussion of current issues such as mental disorders, addiction, and AIDS.

Ratzinger, Joseph. *The Spirit of the Liturgy*. San Francisco: Ignatius, 2000.

This is a rich biblical, theological, and sacramental study of the liturgy. It includes discussions of the role of the Old Testament in the formation of the liturgy, the importance of sacred buildings and sacred time, sacred images and music, liturgy as rite, and the body and liturgy. This should be in the library of anyone interested in a deeper understanding of the liturgy.

INDEX